PRAISE FOR *THE BOOKSELLER AT THE END OF THE WORLD*

'An extraordinary story.'

— Shaun Bythell, author of *The Diary of a Bookseller*

'Shaw can write about these peaks and troughs [of her life] without a skerrick of maudlin introspection or mawkishness. Battered and emotionally bruised, she marches on. In a word, dauntless, and it's exactly this quality that makes this memoir so readable.'

— Chris Moore, *New Zealand Listener*

'A fascinating, funny and moving story.'

— Nicky Pellegrino, *New Zealand Woman's Weekly*

'Utterly charming and filled with equal measures of heartbreak and humour, Ruth Shaw's memoir will have you booking the first flight to New Zealand to share a cup of tea at her Wee Bookshops. Shaw has been a cook, a nurse, sailor and world traveller, and endured immeasurable loss. But with Lance, the love of her life, Shaw has found her place bookselling in Fiordland.'

— Booksellers' Choice Australia

'Shaw's writing is pragmatic and restrained; her voice is so strong and assured that when grief appears you gasp at its intrusion and your heart stops a second.'

— Alexa Dretzke, Readings Hawthorn

'Amazing!' — Jack Tame, Newstalk ZB

'Compelling. Shaw tells her own story free of oversentimentality or self-pity; she's straightforward, frequently humorous, but, understandably, sometimes guarded and reluctant to overshare. Her resilience, optimism and willingness to always help others is to be admired; her remarkable story is to be read and reflected upon as it adds another vital perspective to a New Zealand life.'

— Dionne Christian, *Sunday Star-Times*

'Ruth describes her experiences with such a straight-up heart, pouring facts and feelings onto the page, that the reader becomes immersed . . . The story wends and weaves until eventually we meet Ruth as she is today . . . to get there with her we go on a hell of a ride.'

— Louise Ward, Wardini Books

'Ruth Shaw's shocking, honest, and ultimately redemptive autobiography is one of the finest I've read. I am in awe of Ruth's ability to write so fearlessly.'

— Peta Stavelli, NZ Booklovers

THREE WEE BOOKSHOPS AT THE END OF THE WORLD

RUTH SHAW

First published in 2025

Allen & Unwin
Level 2, 10 College Hill, Freemans Bay
Auckland 1011, New Zealand
+64 (9) 377 3800
auckland@allenandunwin.com
www.allenandunwin.co.nz

83 Alexander Street
Crows Nest NSW 2065, Australia
+61 (2) 8425 0100

A catalogue record for this book is available from the National Library of New Zealand.

ISBN 978 1 991006 55 4

Design by Saskia Nicol and Katrina Duncan
Cover illustration and endpapers by Sophie Watson
Printed by C&C Offset Printing Co. Ltd, China

10 9 8 7 6 5 4 3 2

This book is for Jo and Nelson, Sally and Jenny, Wilma and Renee, and Jeongeun.

CONTENTS

PROLOGUE

How many times did my husband Lance urge me to write my story? I can't recall, but it was mentioned frequently over the years. Yet it wasn't until I was approached by Jenny Hellen from Allen & Unwin that I finally found the confidence to start writing seriously.

I had thick files of short stories I had written since I was 20 years old. I wrote children's stories for the newspaper in New Guinea when I lived in Rabaul; I won a short story competition in New South Wales, then a few years later a story about learning to dive won me an incredible diving adventure for two on the Queensland coast.

For our family I wrote stories about my childhood, and my aunties and uncles. I diligently kept diaries in my tiny handwriting, sometimes with drawings, and with leaves, flowers and bus and train tickets pressed between the pages.

Yes, I could write, but was I good enough to write a whole book that people would want to read? Jenny obviously thought so, as she emailed me a contract! Lance was delighted. Jenny in her wisdom suggested I have a support person, who turned out to be Emma Clifton, a talented local journalist/writer. I dived in, and once a month Emma and I went through what I had written, sometimes sharing tears, other times laughter.

I had no confidence that *The Bookseller at the End of the World* would do well. It is the brilliant team at Allen & Unwin that I must thank for the fact that it became a best-seller. Now the book has been translated into 12 languages. I can still hardly believe it.

I realised the impact *The Bookseller* was making when increasing numbers of people started to turn up at my Wee Bookshops in Manapōuri wanting to buy a copy, or bringing their own copy to be signed. Suddenly it seemed I was 'known' — recognised as a writer at the age of 75!

It wasn't just New Zealanders — some overseas travellers told me they planned their whole holiday around when my shops would be open so they could meet me! What started as a few visitors soon turned into a torrent and I have had to employ help in the shops. Phil, a local retired gentleman with a wealth of local knowledge and a love of books, works for me a few days a week. Lance also now works in the shops nearly every day during the season. 'Lovely Lance' (as he is sometimes called by the ladies) happily has his photo taken too.

Then there is Dylan, now in the third year of his bookshop 'apprenticeship'. He started with me when he was 13. Even back then his aim in life was to own a bookshop. And now there is Sarah, a book lover/reader/collector who works one or more days a week.

As the shops are so busy during the season, housework is not on my 'to do' list. Veronika is my fabulous housekeeper and 'do anything' lady. Every week she arrives with a huge smile and spends a few hours restoring order around our home.

How has all of this changed my life? Well, it's been huge. I get multiple hugs and have my photo taken numerous times a day. Letters and emails arrive daily. I reply to every one as I cannot thank my readers enough for their thoughtfulness.

With the support of Allen & Unwin we have sent copies of *The Bookseller* to the 40 Women's Refuges in New Zealand, and also to the two women's prisons. I am humbled that so many women — and men — come and tell me their stories about forced adoption, rape, divorce, loss of a child, and broken marriages. There are often tears, but there is also a lot of laughter — and of course there are hugs.

Readers started asking early on for a follow-up memoir, but I wasn't ready to write the second part of my life story, so I wrote *Bookshop Dogs*. That was a fun project. Dogs and books — what a fabulous combination. Photographer Graham Dainty was always on hand to get a special photo, and between us we produced another bestseller. People now turn up at the Wee Bookshops with their dogs and I get a rush of happiness every time I get to hug and pat a new dog.

—

AT THE AGE of 65, in 2011, I married for the fourth time, becoming Mrs Ruth Shaw.

The year before, Lance and I had sold our businesses — Fiordland Ecology Holidays and the associated bookshop 45 South and Below — and retired.

Every winter for the next six years we travelled — holidaying all over the world. Lance bought a Noelex 22 and got back into yacht racing. My son built us a beautiful new bathroom overlooking our big back yard, and I busied myself in our small forest and became passionately involved (again) in fighting for the environment.

But the word 'retirement' is problematic, to my mind. The word 'tire' suggests a loss of energy — you have reached an age where you are exhausted by life and need to sit back and relax.

Lance told our friends he was studying the art of retirement and was determined to graduate. He was doing well, but after six years I knew I was failing the challenge. I tried, I really did, but the thought of opening another bookshop kept niggling in my head.

When I could no longer ignore it, the decision was made and the first Wee Bookshop arrived on the back of a large trailer. The perfect location was on our land, right beside our home, on the corner of Home Street and Hillside Road in Manapōuri.

I was back among shelves of wonderful books: I was happy, busy and *not* retired.

When I had packed up the books from 45 South in 2010, with the help of friends, I wasn't able to bring myself to sell them or give them away so I stowed them. Our home was exploding with bookshelves groaning under the weight of all the books I had kept. Lance had drawn a line: no bookshelves in the bedroom. I honoured this, but the result was growing piles of books on both sides of our bed — Lance is an avid reader like me.

Now suddenly, in 2016, all these books had a home. My Wee Bookshop in time morphed into two, and then three, a sure sign of chronic bibliophilia.

The Wee Bookshops are open from the end of September to the middle of April. For the other four months of the year I am sourcing books to fill empty shelves, catching up on reading, and racing around the country attending book festivals and other events organised by Abba from Allen & Unwin, and writing. Not very retired . . .

AUTUMN IS HERE, the air is damp; it is time to close the shops for winter. I pack up all the children's books, checking them off on the database. The soft toys I keep in the shop are tucked into a big box, then I lock the small red door.

I repeat the process with The Snug, the third and smallest of the three shops. Fishing, hunting, war, farming, tractor and train books are checked off the database and stowed for the winter.

I set up a dehumidifier in the main shop and turn a small oil heater on low. I lock the door and the three once-obscure Wee Bookshops are in hibernation until spring.

I tingle with excitement as I now have time to write.

'When is your next book coming out, Ruth?'

This question has been asked nearly every day.

So, dear readers, here it is, the sequel to *The Bookseller at the End of the World*.

This period of my life was not as chaotic as my first 35 years, but there were still many tears, and there were still a lot of laughs. Welcome back into my world.

Let's get on with it, shall we?

CHAPTER
1

THE AUCKLAND TO SUVA YACHT RACE

My first book ended in 1985 when I found Andrew, the beautiful blond boy I had given up for adoption 21 years earlier. That meeting will always be one of the most incredible moments of my life. As I wrote, 'Even now, when we talk about our first encounter, the strongest memory we both have is of the instant shared burst of laughter. Andrew has the same laugh and the same big, wide-mouthed-frog smile as me.'

It was a tumultuous time for me. I had reconnected with Lance the previous year, 17 years after we had called off our engagement, to the immense grief of us both. I had been raised a Catholic and he had not, and back then the divide could not be bridged. Now, older and wiser, we happily picked up where we had left off.

—

IN LATE APRIL 1985 Lance and I joined the crew of the yacht *Shaylene*, owned by Les and Olive Hutchins, founders of Fiordland Travel (now RealNZ). We were to compete in a field of 30 yachts in the Auckland to Suva yacht race, in the cruising yacht division.

Shaylene was a 55-foot (16.8-metre) steel cutter built as a cruising motor sailer, with a 6LW Gardner diesel engine. There were eight of us in the crew. The only two with racing experience were Lance and Graham. Four of us had blue-water sailing experience but this was to be everyone's first ocean race. We would be lining up for the start on Saturday 4 May.

The Royal Akarana Yacht Club has been the base for blue-water offshore racing from as early as 1931 with the trans-Tasman race. The first Auckland to Suva race, over a distance of 1100 nautical miles, was held in 1956. Line honours that year went to a yacht named *Wanderer*, which completed the race in 11 days, 12 hours, 26 minutes.

To familiarise ourselves with *Shaylene*, her sails and how she handled, we were out in the Hauraki Gulf by 10 a.m. the next morning. Les proudly announced that he had bought a new multi-purpose sail (MPS), which we hoisted with great difficulty. Les went pale watching us struggle to handle it.

The next few days were extremely busy. Several items of gear were needed: a new mirror for the sextant, nautical flags as required by the race committee, spare shackles, batteries and ropes, a comprehensive first-aid kit, safety harnesses, food supplies, crystals for the radio, and an emergency position indicator radio beacon (EPIRB).

Les had had a huge bus bench seat made to fit across the width of the yacht above the aft cabin. It fitted perfectly, but of major concern was that we could no longer easily use the winches to work the sails. Instead of winching in a 360-degree movement we had to reduce this to 180 degrees, while continually knocking our knuckles on the blasted bench seat. As a joke I collected a number of used bus tickets and handed them out to the crew, explaining that without a ticket they would not be permitted to sit on Les's bench seat, as it proved to be the most popular seat on board.

Meanwhile, other crews were offloading gear they didn't require on board for the race, making their vessels as light as possible . . .

The crew of *Urban Cowboy* had a pile of pre-made sandwiches for their meals. We had at least eight boiled chickens, along with salad ingredients, fresh vegetables, piles of fruit, frozen desserts and even after-dinner mints.

Les had smart T-shirts made, which we wore proudly to the pre-race meeting held at the yacht club, where safety was high on the agenda. As we shook hands with other boats' crew members you could feel the anticipation in the air. Some of them had obviously been watching us and someone asked if we were one of the race committee boats! Perhaps it was our stylish bench seat . . .

Lance was officially made sail captain. Les was overall skipper and navigator, I was the radio operator and in charge of first aid, and we were all to help with cooking. Two crew on each watch, set for two hours on and six hours off — how easy was that?

Race day — 4 May

Perfect weather, and with the MPS up we even managed to pass a few boats. The race was on. Five out of the eight of us were seasick within the first few hours, even though we had taken seasickness tablets. As usual, I also had diarrhoea — I asked everyone on deck to face for'ard while I hung my bare bum over the aft rail.

Lance, an avid yacht racer, was intent on sailing *Shaylene* as hard as he could. Then the next crew on watch would slacken off the sails to reduce the list, which meant slowing the boat down. I lay in my bunk furious that we went from racing to cruising mode depending on who was on watch.

The winds increased in strength and as *Shaylene* was a heavy boat she handled the rough weather well. *Al Fresco* had to withdraw due to a steering problem, *Paneka*, which was leading our division, was dismasted, and *Kismet* was now leading overall.

Radio schedule 0725: we had lost two placings overnight and were now down to sixth on handicap. Lance announced to all: 'No more holidays, all rags up, we are now seriously racing.'

All of the competing yachts had to radio in their positions each day. The wind had dropped considerably so we were only managing 4–6 knots. *Nova* was in big trouble — she had lost her rudder and some of the crew had serious seasickness so they withdrew from the race.

We tried everything to get a few more knots out of the sails, including loose-footing the staysail, as the MPS was continually wrapping itself around the forestay and not setting properly. We had just freed the sail from the forestay for the fifth time when a gust of wind blew the sail out, causing us to jibe — there was total chaos until Lance sorted us out. Les was speechless as his new MPS sail was now damaged. On the radio we heard the other boats confirm that they were enjoying great racing conditions under spinnakers, but we had no spinnaker in our sail wardrobe.

Day 7

Lance and I were on watch 0600 to 0800. The radio schedule at 0725 showed we were now fifth in our division. Lance was keen to up our game so we set about hand-stitching the ripped MPS. The entire foot of the sail and all around the clew was torn. Luckily, I had my leather palm and sail repair kit with me, and three of us worked steadily for several hours on the repair.

Meanwhile, the others were constantly changing sails in an attempt to get as much performance as possible out of them while everyone waited for the MPS to be repaired. Graham, Lance and Dave were trying to pole out the genoa when suddenly the wind changed direction and the pole crashed across the foredeck into the sidestay. Dave's hand was caught between the pole and the sidestay.

'My finger is off!' Dave shouted.

I grabbed my T-shirt off the rail where it was drying, raced across to him and wrapped it around his damaged, bloody hand. I led him below and lay him on a bunk, calling out for the first-aid kit while I checked his hand. Two fingers on his left hand were severely broken and torn, with one being held on only by a flap of skin. I sedated Dave as best I could and cleaned up his hand, placing the fingers back into position. I strapped and bandaged the whole hand and wrapped two packets of frozen peas over the bandages. Lance helped me set up a sling from the bunk above Dave's, so we could keep his arm elevated.

I tried to radio the Suva Yacht Club and Suva Radio to notify them of the accident and request immediate assistance but could not raise them. Yacht *Spyker* called us and agreed to relay for us. After a very short wait a doctor from the Suva Yacht Club came through loud and clear. I explained what I had done and how much medication I had given Dave. He agreed that there was little else I could do on board, but unfortunately no medical operations were carried out in Suva on weekends unless it was a life-or-death situation.

Our next option was to get him onto the first possible flight to Auckland so his finger could be reattached. We notified Suva that we were out of racing mode and would be motoring towards an island where we hoped a helicopter or float-plane could meet us.

The one helicopter available was $1000 an hour but didn't have lifting gear, so that wasn't an option. It had to be a float-plane. Dave was still asleep — heavily sedated — but his temperature was rising so I placed ice packs wrapped in a towel on his forehead.

Then suddenly we had a new problem — the main engine locked up. Unbeknown to us, the exhaust system had been back-filling and had flooded the whole engine.

Graham, Les and Lance worked on the engine for six hours. They removed the sump plug and drained the oil and water from the engine. To clear the water from the cylinders they used the forward movement of the boat to slowly turn the propeller, which bled the water out. Thankfully it was a reliable Gardner, and just after midnight it was running sweetly again.

We headed for Fiji's Kadavu Island, where we had arranged to meet the float-plane at 1015 the next day. All going well, Dave would be flown to Nadi to meet the Air New Zealand flight to Auckland departing at 1400. Auckland Hospital had been notified and he would be rushed straight into surgery on arrival there.

Most of us went to bed at 0400 exhausted, while Les and Olive stood watch. We aimed to be on anchor at Kadavu Island by 0800.

Day 8

We were all up at 0630. Dave was in excellent spirits, chatting and laughing, the perfect patient. I changed his dressing and was pleased to see the bleeding had stopped and his fingers were still in place.

We anchored in the arranged position with time to spare. At 1010 we spotted the float-plane flying towards us, but then it veered off and headed south. We tried to radio the pilot but had no response. We waited to see if the plane would return but after 20 stressful minutes there was still no sign of him. Dave was the only one of us who seemed relaxed — he was even cracking jokes! Suva Radio told us they had also lost contact with the pilot.

After 35 minutes the small plane reappeared on the horizon and we fired off numerous flares to attract the pilot's attention — not that we would have been hard to find, as we were the only yacht in the anchorage.

At last the radio came alive. The pilot was reluctant to land close to us and asked if we could use the life-raft to bring Dave alongside him where he landed. We were reluctant to deploy the large, 10-person life-raft for this purpose when we thought it unnecessary.

Lance took over the radio and explained that he had a lot of experience with float-planes landing beside our vessel in Fiordland. 'Just land and come nose first on the starboard side,' he said. 'Lines are prepared for you.' After a long hesitation the pilot agreed. Everything went smoothly — we transferred Dave onto the plane, waved him goodbye and notified Suva Radio that he was on his way.

We were told we could re-enter the race at 1230 so we hoisted the repaired MPS, which thankfully held its shape as it filled with wind. We were back in business.

We anticipated finishing the race at 2400, midnight. Sailing conditions were excellent, but as the tide was running out, we had to tack several times to sail through the passage. I was stationed up on the bow listening for waves crashing on the reef. When the reef sounded close I shouted, 'Tack!', and on this command the crew brought *Shaylene* through the wind and settled her on the opposite tack. It was stressful and dangerous; under normal circumstances we would have stood off for the night.

We crossed the finish line at 0149.

—

THE WONDERFUL NEWS the next day was that both of Dave's fingers had been saved. We were all ecstatic. I wrote to the *Fiji Times* and the *Suva Sun* to thank everyone for helping us get Dave to Auckland and to let them know the outcome.

On the race awards night we were told *Shaylene* had been disqualified; I can't remember the reason anymore, but at the time it was disappointing. *Urban Cowboy*, with the crew of young guys who lived on sandwiches for the whole race, won line honours: 5 days, 8 hours, 53 seconds. This was less than half the time recorded by *Wanderer* in 1956.

I was shocked when the commodore of the Royal Akarana Yacht Club then called me to come up the front. He told the story of Dave's accident and presented me with a small travelling clock. *Shaylene* and her crew received some limelight after all.

—

OUR ENGINE REQUIRED a replacement part, which was to be delivered to the boat. When the time came to go ashore for dinner the part had still not arrived, so Les offered to stay behind to wait for it and join us later.

'No,' exclaimed Lance quickly. 'Ruth and I will wait for the part. No hassle, Les.'

'You don't need to do that,' Les replied, but Lance was adamant so we stayed behind.

The rest of the crew left and Lance and I were at last alone together for the first time in nearly two weeks on board.

We made our way up to the for'ard cabin. The only place with enough room for us to lie down together was on the deck between the bunks, with our feet stuck out into the saloon. We were soon oblivious to everything, making the most of this precious time to ourselves. The arrival of an engine part was low in our priorities.

When we returned to the saloon we saw the motor part on the table. Oops! Whoever had dropped it off would not have been able to miss four feet protruding from under the curtain. Oh well, what a story he had to tell his mates!

We headed off to meet up with Les and the rest of the crew. 'Part arrived, Les,' Lance said matter-of-factly.

'What did they say?'

'Nothing.'

'They must have said something when they dropped it off.'

'Nope, just dropped it off.'

Les shook his head. 'Very strange.'

It was a long time before we told him the full story.

TALES FROM THE BOOKSHOPS: THE UROLOGY BOOKSHOP

THE FIRST WEE BOOKSHOP was a standalone, colourful little cabin with about 700 books. It needed a name. You would think that a wordsmith could come up with something catchy, but I just couldn't. As usual, I was in a rush, and I needed a name immediately, so it was just called the Wee Bookshop.

When the Children's Bookshop arrived and was placed just a few paces away from the first, they became the Two Wee Bookshops.

No matter where I go, people refer to them as the Two Wee Bookshops, reinforcing the mantra 'Keep it simple'. I have been open now for eight years and customers have told me they have done an online search, getting as far as Two Wee . . . and there they are, before they even type in the last word. Quite famous now, it seems.

It wasn't until Lance and I were staying with some dear friends in Wellington, Lisa and Jonathan, that I had a moment's doubt about the name. They both love books. This is confirmed by the number of fully stacked bookshelves throughout their house, even in the toilet, where I settled to reading *The Big Little Book of Jewish Wit & Wisdom* by Sally Ann Berk. It was the perfect book to read while sitting on a warm toilet seat, and yes, there was a lot of wisdom tucked away in the pages:

He who has fed a stranger may have fed an angel.

If your wife is short, bend down and listen to her.

Both are from the Talmud, which is a collection of teachings from the fourth and fifth centuries regarded as sacred by Jews.

Lisa is a bookseller who works at Unity Books in Wellington. Jonathan, who is Jewish, is one of New Zealand's top palliative care specialists and oozes empathy. We share a similar sense of humour, which some may consider sharp, if not rude. It should not have come as a shock to me when Jonathan asked, 'Wee Bookshops! Is that where urologists go to find books?'

I punched his arm. 'I will never be able to think of my bookshops in the same way again! It will always be about urologists and wees now!'

CHAPTER
2

BREAKTHROUGH ON BREAKSEA ISLAND

I didn't realise until after my grandfather had died that he was, in many ways, a conservationist. When he took us fishing in Lyttelton Harbour from a very young age we learnt to take only what we could eat. If we wanted the pipi beds and rock oysters to thrive, we would harvest just enough for the family.

So it is not surprising that I grew up caring about our environment and taking a stand when I felt it needed to be done. My first protest march was in Auckland in 1964, and it was the first of many. My life, and the way I live, has long been centred on the environment.

The battle to eradicate rats from Breaksea Island in the 1980s was definitely one of the highlights for me. I only played a small part, but we won, and today the native flora and fauna flourish there as a result.

It started back in 1964 when the Wildlife Service received a report that there had been an explosion of rats on Taukihepa or Big South Cape Island, off the south-west corner of Stewart Island/Rakiura. This was a huge risk to the flocks of sooty shearwaters, also known as tītī or muttonbirds, and many other seabirds that reared their chicks in well-established earth burrows there. Big South Cape Island was recognised as one of the last safe havens for many of New Zealand's endangered flora and fauna species, including the South Island saddleback and the greater short-tailed bat.

It was thought that rats had first arrived on a mutton-birders' boat early in the 1960s, and within a few years they had devastated the previously predator-free island, pushing Stead's bush wren, the South Island snipe and the greater short-tailed bat to extinction.

Ornithologist Don Merton had spent a month on the island for the Wildlife Service three years before the rat outbreak, and therefore was in a good position to assess the impact of the rat infestation. He and Brian Bell, together with a small team, were given the job of visiting the island to investigate.

They found that the wallpaper in the huts had been

stripped of its flour-based paste by ravenous rats, but that was nothing to what had occurred in the forest. Young trees had been stripped of bark, small bushes had been eaten to ground level, and many insect species, including the giant wētā, had vanished. The last few bush wrens were transferred to a small enclosure for refuge but this desperate attempt to rescue the tiny, near-flightless bird failed. By 1972 the tiny bush wren no longer existed.

—

WHEN DON MERTON was a young scientist the flightless kākāpō was thought to be doomed to extinction. A few male birds were found in Fiordland in the 1970s, but no females. When a few female birds were eventually found, Merton led the recovery and relocation effort that everyone hoped would ensure the species' survival. It did: in 2023 there were 247 kākāpō known to be in existence.

Merton dedicated his life to saving many of Aotearoa's rare and endangered birds, including the black robin. Five individuals were found living on Māngere Island off Chatham Island. Wildlife officials named the single female Old Blue. During her long life she raised 11 chicks, ensuring that black robins would continue to exist. When she died at the ripe old age of about 13 her death was announced in Parliament with a minute's silence. This incredible story is among many recorded in David Butler and Don Merton's book *The Black Robin: Saving the World's Most Endangered Bird.*

—

DESPITE THE ECOLOGICAL DISASTER on Taukihepa/Big South Cape Island in 1964, it was not until 1976 that 57 leading wildlife authorities met in Wellington to discuss the control of rodents in nature reserves. By then the Norway or brown rat, the black ship rat and the smaller kiore were all contributing to the demise of our native flora and fauna, especially birds. Kiore came to New Zealand with early Māori voyagers, while the other species arrived on whaling ships and with early European settlers.

A young wildlife technician, Bruce Thomas, was at that meeting and he listened intently as his interest was rats! When he was young he had tried to eliminate rats on his family farm. Early in his wildlife career he met Rowley Taylor, who was also trapping rats. Both worked for the Department of Scientific and Industrial Research (DSIR) Ecology Division. Taylor was pessimistic about the elimination of rats from New Zealand bush, but Thomas was an eternal optimist. When he visited Breaksea Island off the Fiordland coast in the early 1980s he found it overrun with brown rats. Would it be possible to get rid of them all?

The rugged and densely vegetated 170-hectare Breaksea Island lies at the mouth of Breaksea Sound, one of the southern fiords. Just east of this main island is the smaller Hāwea Island, which also had a rat problem. In 1986 Thomas and Taylor chose the smaller island as the location of a radical experiment. It was proven to be outside the swimming range of stoats, and there were no possums. If they could rid the island of Norway rats it would be a huge achievement for conservation.

An agricultural chemist in the UK had come up with a new poison, brodifacoum, registered under the name of Talon. The plan was to use the rats' own community network to carry the poison back to their nest sites.

Hāwea Island, at just under 9 hectares, was an ideal size for their experiment, which began in March 1986. They covered the island in trails, and every 40 metres or so they placed some poison in a length of drainage pipe — 73 bait stations in all.

Lance was involved with the project from the beginning as he was skippering the Department of Conservation's vessel *Renown*, which was not only a means of transport for teams of scientists and volunteers but also offered accommodation.

A week later there were no rats left on Hāwea Island.

Breaksea Island was now on their radar. Despite facing a funding shortfall, Taylor and Thomas organised supplies, volunteers, a hut and helicopter time. Young volunteers from Operation Raleigh in the United Kingdom arrived to assist, with no idea that the island where they would be working and living was so isolated, as well as being in the middle of a rainforest and home to millions of sandflies (known as blackflies elsewhere; Captain Cook used the word sandfly in his log, and it has stuck in New Zealand).

The team had no idea how long the eradication would take, so they guessed about three weeks. The DSIR and the newly minted Department of Conservation offered only limited funding to the project but individual staff pulled strings where they could to assist. A local fisherman delivered food supplies to the island, often adding little surprises for the volunteers, and the odd newspaper.

Lance knew where there were coils of old cray-pot rope that would be perfect for the volunteers' purposes. Some of the tracks were established on steep rocky slopes where it was essential to have guide ropes to hang on to. Ernie Cave, from the fishing boat *Hustler*, was dropping off supplies one day and recognised some rope as coming from his cray-pots. He suggested that Lance replace his old cray-pot rope with coils of 14-mm polypropylene to settle the score.

By the end of April 1988 some 743 pieces of drainage pipe had been placed at 50-metre intervals, all within sniffing distance of a rat. On 24 May we left Doubtful Sound on the *Renown* for the last push — setting the bait stations. I was lucky enough to be the third crew member, helping with the cooking and doing anything else I could to ensure the project was a success.

Bruce Thomas had calculated that they would need around 350 kg of poison, most of which was donated by the manufacturers. A team of six volunteers baited all the stations, which were checked and reloaded with bait every day. The number of poison baits taken from each station was recorded — they were being taken as quickly as they could be replenished.

Over the next few days the blue pins on the map marking stations where bait was disappearing were overtaken by red pins showing where the bait remained untouched. Rowley Taylor physically monitored some of the bait stations and observed large male rats waiting for new bait to arrive, then carrying it to their nests after eating as much as they could on site.

By day 20 only one blue pin remained. There was at least one rat still alive, but we were committed to leaving the next day. All the stations were rebaited with two poison baits and an apple apiece. Then we steamed out of Breaksea Sound and up the coast to Doubtful Sound, all feeling extremely positive that we had won the Battle of Breaksea.

A month later we returned to Breaksea Island to find the bait and the apples all still in place. We now had the evidence the island was rat free. This conservation triumph was down to the determination of Rowley Taylor and Bruce Thomas and their team of dedicated volunteers. Around the world many other rat-infested islands went on to gain predator-free status by copying the Breaksea blueprint.

—

YEARS LATER, WHEN we set up Fiordland Ecology Holidays, Lance travelled to Queensland to purchase the buckeye ketch *Reef Explorer*. He sailed her home to New Zealand where we wanted to rename her. Sitting around a table with some friends and our crew we decided she should be called *Breaksea Girl*.

As no government funding was available for ongoing monitoring of predator-free Breaksea Island, Lance and I decided we would subsidise a six-day expedition every year, led by Taylor and Thomas, to record the rehabilitation of the flora and fauna.

A small group of passengers paid for the privilege of helping to carry out this important work. Incredibly, the same people signed up year after year. They came from different walks of life but all were united in their purpose and got caught up in the rewarding work of counting birds, penguins and knobbled weevils, and witnessing the return of a healthy forest.

What we got away with back then would horrify health and safety experts today. We counted weevils at night, jumping from the dinghy onto rocky outcrops with our headlamps on. We leapt from the dinghy to the shore in brutal weather conditions, and took all sorts of other calculated risks. We did this for 12 years.

We all owe a huge debt to the first hardy volunteers who

set up camp on Breaksea Island to cut the tracks and set the bait stations.

Since the successful rat eradication, Breaksea Island has been used for the translocation of several rare bird species, including tieke (saddlebacks) and mōhua (yellowheads). Other reintroductions have included Fiordland skinks and knobbled weevils. (We took what I think may be the only photo of knobbled weevils mating.)

Beetle, wētā and spider populations boomed, and Fiordland crested penguins re-established nesting sites.

Seabird scientist Graeme Taylor was on one of our trips and he spent some time exploring the Gilbert Islands, further south of Breaksea. One day he came back on board excited to tell us he had just found the northernmost breeding site of the broad-billed prion. Lance and Peter, his crew, kept very quiet about having previously discovered the prions breeding on Wairaki, one of the smaller islands off Breaksea Island.

The next day they made a sign and placed it on Wairaki, reading: 'Northernmost breeding site of the broad-billed prion'. Without saying a word, they dropped Graeme off on the far side of Wairaki for a half-day's exploring. It was arranged that he would be picked up on the other side of the island, where the sign had been placed. His language was apparently colourful when he read the sign, but he did enjoy the joke.

I was cook/crew on many of the Breaksea trips. I now

look back in amazement at the incredible hurdles we faced, most of us aged in our 50s and 60s at the time. We became lifelong friends with the team of volunteers who returned annually for 12 years, and still relish our contribution to what was at the time truly a conservation triumph.

The Natural History Unit of Television New Zealand in Dunedin produced a short documentary film titled *Battle for Breaksea* in 1989, which can be viewed on the *New Zealand Geographic* website.

For anyone interested in rat eradication on various islands around the world I highly recommend *Rat Island: Predators in Paradise and the World's Greatest Wildlife Rescue* by William Stolzenburg, published in 2012 by Bloomsbury.

TALES FROM THE BOOKSHOPS: THE NEW OLD DESK

MY OLD OFFICE DESK had been with me for over 25 years. In that time there was hardly a day when I did not sit down and work at it. I changed computers and printers, but never my desk.

Until!

I was looking for another small bookshelf, so went to see Steve and Vicky, who own Time Traders, the fabulous second-hand/antique shop here in Manapōuri. I couldn't find what I wanted so Steve suggested I visit them at their home after hours. He said he had something he thought I would be interested in.

When we arrived, Steve showed us a wonderful rotating circular library with wooden slats, but that wasn't what I was looking for either. We went into the large garage where all their surplus stock is stored, and where Steve repairs, cleans, polishes and restores the treasures they find before they are put into the shop.

Standing apart from the general clutter was a beautiful teak desk that Steve had just finished working on. The woodwork was incredible — in fact I thought it was magnificent.

'Time you had a really nice desk, love,' Lance said to me as he ran his hand over the wood. 'Why don't we buy it?'

'The desk I have is fine.'

'But look at how beautiful it is! You deserve to have a desk like this.'

Steve pointed to a small metal tag fixed to the front of the desk. It read:

Presented to: F G HALL-JONES. Esq.
The Southland Progress League Inc.
April 1946

'The year I was born!' I exclaimed. 'This has to be John Hall-Jones's father.'

John Hall-Jones was a dear friend who we nicknamed 'Shorts', as that was his attire, no matter what the season. He was an ear, nose and throat surgeon who worked at Southland Hospital for 30 years. When he retired he pursued his passion for books, becoming the respected author of 34 historical books, among them *Early Fiordland* (1968), *Mr Surveyor Thomson* (1971), *Pioneers of Te Anau* (1983) and *Goldfields of Otago* (2005). He carried out his research by exploring the wilderness in the region he wanted to write about, sometimes flying, often kayaking, trekking or camping. He died in 2015 at the age of 88.

John's father, Frederick George Hall-Jones (owner of the fine desk), was born near Timaru in 1891. He was a lawyer, and also an author. His titles included *King of the Bluff* (1943), *Historical Southland* (1945), *Invercargill Pioneers* (1946) and *Early Timaru* (1956).

And Frederick's father, Sir William Hall-Jones, a former builder, served briefly as New Zealand Prime Minister in 1906, then later as high commissioner to London. He was knighted in 1910.

But back to the desk . . .

'We *have* to buy it, Lance,' I said. 'John would love us to have it.'

Everyone agreed. Within three days my old desk was on the local community market website, and my wonderful new desk was set up ready for work. This is where I sit to write, surrounded by paper, books, pens and pencils, a printer and a soft-toy guinea pig that Lance bought me.

It is unbelievable that this beautiful desk from such an interesting and important family has found its way to our place. So many books may well have been written by both Frederick and John at this desk. When I sit down to write, I start by silently acknowledging two famous writers.

Hello, John and Fred. Here we go on another writing adventure.

I am sitting where they sat.

CHAPTER 3

BACK TO DARKNESS

Now is a good time to write this as I feel sad, and this is a sad story. Being sad is a time when your heart feels heavy, hidden tears build up awaiting release, and you notice there is a slight tremble in your hands and voice.

I was exhausted, unable to sleep. My only release was to bury myself in work and push aside what I feared was happening. I was on the road to another mental collapse. Three years after reconnecting, Lance and I were struggling to live together — we loved each other but it just wasn't enough. I lived in fear that I would sabotage our relationship, unable mentally or physically to settle down.

We actually only lived together for about four months a

year, as Lance was away at sea the rest of the time. We both had jobs that we loved but that demanded long periods apart. We'd have a few days together and then Lance was off to sea and I was back to being a youth worker on the streets of Invercargill. We just could not get into the rhythm of it.

We knew deep down that we loved each other and wanted to be together, but was that enough?

One day a council vehicle was sweeping our street — clearing the gutters, spraying stones onto the grass verges. I snapped. Blindly I raced out onto the road and stood in front of the vehicle, screaming, totally out of control.

'You are not going to clear in front of our place!'

The vehicle stopped just a few metres in front of me. The driver glared at me through his windscreen, shaking his head and then waving his hand at the footpath. I didn't move.

Lance came out to see what was happening. 'Ruth, why are you screaming? Come back inside. He's just doing his job. It's just a few stones.'

I turned reluctantly and went back inside, sobbing, my mind blank.

'I have had enough, Ruth,' said Lance. 'This has been building up for months — you need help. Either you agree to seeing someone or I'm leaving. I can't do this anymore.'

—

HOW HAD IT got this bad? I knew I had switched off emotionally over time, not talking to Lance about how I was feeling, not wanting to be touched but at the same time yearning to be held. Lance was still going through the healing process from losing his son Dane when his wife up and left while he was away at sea. He had come home to an empty house and a letter saying the marriage was over. This was at least a year before I arrived back on the scene.

We went through a honeymoon period when I first came back from Australia to Manapōuri to live with Lance in 1984. He had been my first love, and now, incredibly, we were back together. This was where we wanted to be and we both believed our love was strong enough to make it work. But how could it be, when neither of us had fully addressed what had happened in our lives over the years?

Now here we were at a crossroads. Lance had given me an ultimatum: either I get help or he was leaving. I was back down in the darkness — uncontrollable, scared, switched off — and he didn't know what to do.

Frightened as I was, I decided to seek help. Lance drove me to Kew Hospital in Invercargill, where we pulled up outside Ward 12: Mental Health. Lance explained to the doctor what had been happening over the previous few months, and that I had tried to commit suicide before returning to New Zealand. He believed I was suicidal again. As much as we loved each other, it wasn't working.

'I'm sorry, love,' he said to me. 'I have tried my best but I can't do this anymore.' There was a deep sadness in his eyes as he turned and left, his shoulders shaking as he wept quietly.

WARD 12, KEW HOSPITAL, under suicide watch. What can I remember? Hardly anything except that a nurse was with me all night, and Lance was gone. The days were a blur: eat, sleep, talk to the psychiatrist, attend group therapy, take medication.

After three days I asked for a pen and paper; I had to write. Words began to cover the pages in long garbled sentences. I had never been to counselling before but I knew that now, at the age of 42, it was finally time to start working through everything that had happened to me from the age of 17.

The word 'counsellor' hardly existed when I was raped, or when I had to adopt out my baby son; or when my first husband was killed and then my second son died when he was only a few hours old. Not even when I attempted suicide was it suggested that I talk to someone. All the way through these traumas I convinced myself that I was coping, and later that I could put everything behind me and start a new life with Lance.

Now I knew that if I wanted Lance back in my life I had to finally face my past.

Many years later I discovered that after I had been in Kew Hospital for two weeks the psychiatrist organised a marine radio call with Lance, who was at sea. The doctor told Lance he thought I would never recover if he didn't offer the possibility of us getting back together, and as I had agreed to continue counselling he was confident we could work it out.

When Lance returned from sea he came down to Invercargill to speak to the psychiatrist, after which he agreed to see me. I sensed his reluctance to discuss our future together — he was desperately clinging to his own sanity, let alone having to consider taking me back into his life. But in true Lance manner he agreed to try, to give us another chance.

Ensuring support was in place, hospital staff eventually said I could go home, but not to return to work. I was to attend group therapy sessions and see the psychiatrist on a regular basis. Slowly my medication was reduced, and I accepted that I needed long-term counselling. When I was driven back to Manapōuri I was anxious and fearful but also hopeful, as I had started to address what was causing my depression, and my constant need to run.

When the car stopped outside our home in Manapōuri I saw that the footpath was covered in red rose petals. Lance had asked our neighbours if he could raid their huge rose garden. He was desperate to show me that he was willing to do anything to make me happy. I was overwhelmed as

I walked along the path into Lance's open arms. We held each other, weeping. I knew this was where I wanted to be.

—

THANKFULLY THIS STORY has a happy ending, but it wasn't easy. It took time, a lot of tears, and fearless honesty about everything. No topic was out of bounds.

I had promised my doctor that one of the first issues I would address was finding a resting place for the wooden cross I had taken from my baby son's grave in Brisbane. Joshua had rhesus disease and died 13 hours after he was born. He was buried in the paupers' section of a cemetery. Years later I went back to visit his grave. Overwhelmed, I pulled the cross out of the ground, and for the following seven years I lugged it everywhere with me. Finally I placed it in storage, awaiting a time when I would settle down in one place.

As Lance's and my relationship began to heal we still stumbled from time to time, but I had learnt how to pick myself up. When we were both convinced that Manapōuri was my home, I began to look for a resting place for Joshua's cross. The doctor talked to council staff on my behalf and found the perfect place, overlooking the Te Anau basin, with a view across to the mountains. A small brass plaque reads: 'Joshua, 13 hours old, finally at rest.'

I had set myself goals and was determined to remain

positive. There was no way I wanted to experience the heavy feeling of depression again. Sadness yes, maybe anxiety and even fear, but not the blackness of depression.

I stopped spring-cleaning the house every week, and no longer did I iron everything, including Lance's under-pants. Our house turned into a home, and we were happy. My focus was on how much I loved Lance, and in return he surrounded me with unconditional love.

CHAPTER
4

WHO WERE YOU, RITA?

I want to pop in here a little story about a woman called Rita, who I met in 1970.

I was working in a retirement home in New South Wales. Night shift involved checking on the residents to ensure they were either asleep or safely tucked up in bed with their bedside light on, maybe reading or just quietly drifting into and out of their own world of remembrance.

Rita was in a room of her own. The only photo on her set of drawers was of her late husband, handsome in his military uniform, a cheeky smile on his clean-shaven face. Every night when I checked she was awake, sitting up with three pillows supporting her back, the fingers of one hand playing with the top of the blanket as she held a book in the other.

My third night on duty, I asked if she would like to have a cup of tea with me. We could sit together in silence if she wanted. 'I would like that,' she quietly replied.

And so it was that I slowly got to know Rita, who generally kept very much to herself, preferring her own company, immersed in a book that not only entertained her but also formed a barrier between her and the other residents. When I asked the other nurses about her, they said, 'Oh, Rita keeps to herself', or, 'She doesn't want to chat to anyone, she is in her own little world.'

Her medical record was brief: she had been admitted nine months prior, at the age of 82. Born in England in 1888, she had been in the military during the First World War, and married a sergeant from the Australian army who died in 1965. No children or relatives were mentioned. Her health was excellent — the only record of note was that she had had a hysterectomy. Her doctor had admitted her to our elderly care facility after she suffered a number of falls.

Initially Rita and I sat in near silence, drinking our cups of tea with the bedside light on. When we began talking it was often about books, as we both loved reading. I sensed that her long life held many secrets, a burden we shared but did not discuss.

I started to take books in to her. I had just finished *The White Rabbit* by Bruce Marshall, about F.F.E. Yeo-Thomas, a British undercover special agent in the Second World War. With Rita's military service I thought this might interest her.

'I have a great book for you, Rita,' I said as I sat down. 'Finished it early this morning.'

My copy was well read, the card cover creased and some of the pages slightly loose. Rita held it with reverence, the fingers of her right hand caressing the pages.

'I know this book, Ruth. I read it when it was first published and I will certainly enjoy reading it again. What made you read this book?'

'Ever since I read Anne Frank's diary I have been interested in how people survived war, and how brave and courageous many of them were,' I replied. 'I often ask myself if I would have been as brave. I mean, would I be like the White Rabbit or Nancy Wake? Or would I break under torture?'

'None of us know that until we are in that situation,' she replied. 'Sometimes we find courage that we never thought possible.' Rita closed the book and reached for my hand.

Her skin was nearly translucent, the veins prominent, her fingers slightly bent with arthritis. Her fingernails were perfect except for the thumb and forefinger on her right hand, which were scarred and deformed.

Our relationship developed over the following months. We often held hands, and I always kissed her goodnight. It was Rita who led the conversation, asking me questions while avoiding answering my own. I learnt to respect her wish to remain private, even though I was dying to know her story. What did she do during the war? Who was her husband and when did they come to Australia? When and why did she have her hysterectomy?

I had known Rita for nearly a year when I was again on the move, leaving for Sydney. When my last afternoon shift ended I dropped in to say goodbye. We sat, both in tears, clasping hands, not wanting to face our final separation.

'Rita, may I please ask you one question before I go?'

She nodded.

'What were you during the war?'

There was a long silence, her hand trembled and then she sighed. 'I was a radio operator, a spy.' She squeezed my hand. 'Now go, my lovely dear girl.'

'What happened to your hand?' I couldn't resist.

'Only one question!' she answered sternly, and with that she slipped her hand from mine. My last kiss on her forehead was tender. I held her head close to my body, feeling her frailness.

'Thank you,' I whispered, then turned and left.

TALES FROM THE BOOKSHOPS: THE BOOKSELLER'S APPRENTICE

WHEN DYLAN FIRST came to my bookshops he was only 11 years old. Immediately I realised that I was in the presence of a most interesting young man. Catherine, his mother, home-schooled him, so they were able to visit during the week.

Over the time we have known each other, Dylan has grown from a very shy boy to a 15-year-old who looks me in the eye as we discuss interesting and unusual topics.

When I became too busy in the shops, after the publication of *The Bookseller at the End of the World*, I had to look at employing help. Dylan loves books — he is a reader and a collector, and he dreams of a career where he can deal with books every day. Sounded like a budding bookseller to me!

I asked if he would like to work a few hours a week, helping me clean books, keeping the shelves full, sweeping away spiderwebs that reappear daily as I refuse to kill their creators — there were so many small jobs he could do while learning the trade. His answer was 'YES!' He told me he loved spiders and was happy to do anything.

Dylan, who has a form of neurodivergence, turned up for work on the first day, his long hair shining, his dress neat, and carrying a bag containing not only his lunch but also some home baking for us to share at morning teatime.

When the shop was quiet, I told him, 'Just walk around the bookshops and learn where the books are on the shelves. Ask me questions, look at the books, check publishing dates, find out about the authors, read as much as you can.'

Initially he was so shy I did all the talking, but over the season he became extremely knowledgeable and, as his confidence developed, he started to speak to the customers. He can now go through a box of second-hand books on his own: cleaning them, checking that no pages are missing or torn, putting aside any first editions or books signed by authors. He can identify a rare or expensive book and has learnt how to protect them with acid-free, UV-resistant book covering.

He knows how important it is to have the books kept at a relatively even temperature with low humidity. He dusts the books, knows how to stack them on the shelves (leaving a little space between them to reduce the pressure on their spines), and understands the importance of holding a book correctly, especially larger volumes.

Dylan loves old books, no matter what condition they are in. In the book trade, the label 'old' generally refers to a book published before 1830. From this point, printing technology changed so that books could be mass produced, and therefore became more common. So a book that is, say, 100 years old might not have much commercial value if there were a lot of them printed. It may well have sentimental value, of course.

The modern-style dust jacket with flaps was first introduced in the 1830s too (or possibly earlier — the evidence is inconclusive). By the 1870s, dust jackets had become common, though many of them were left blank. In a letter from Lewis Carroll to his publisher in 1876 he requested that the title of his latest book, *The Hunting of the Snark*, be printed on the spine of the 'paper wrapper' so that the book would remain in a 'cleaner and more saleable condition'.

If a valuable hard-covered book has lost its dust jacket it will be devalued, as the dust jacket completes the edition, giving it the final, beautiful publisher's touch. Leather-bound books or books with decorative cloth bindings often have no dust jackets.

Dylan is an eccentric and has the perfect personality to work with books. Now into the third year of his 'apprenticeship', he has been serving customers, looking them in the eye and chatting, something he would never have been able to do when he first started.

'Time for a cup of tea?' he asks me. I nod. He smiles as he goes into the kitchen to make us a well-earned cuppa to go with his homemade biscuits. We talk about books and his dream of owning a bookshop.

CHAPTER
5

DIVING? NO WAY!

Lance had been skippering the *Renown* on the Fiordland coast for a few years when he gained his diving ticket.

The late 1980s and early 1990s were exciting times for divers in Fiordland, where the underwater riches were just beginning to be discovered. Fiordland is a rare marine environment in which a layer of tannin-stained fresh water exists on top of the salt water, blocking out the sunlight. This phenomenon means normally deepwater species can be seen and studied at shallow depths. Marine scientists were arriving from all over the world and on every dive a new underwater critter was discovered.

Marine scientists Ken Grange and R.J. Singleton carried

out ground-breaking research on the black coral colonies in Fiordland. Sea pens were discovered in the Gut, in Doubtful Sound and in Preservation Inlet, together with a new holothurian, named the strawberry holothurian. Scientists were finding new corals, glass sponges, brachiopods and other rock-wall animals.

Ken Grange made the important discovery that the vast majority of marine life in Fiordland existed in the zone between the surface layer and a depth of 40 metres, now known as the 40-metre band. Using this figure and measuring the entire coastline of the fiords, it was calculated that the entire productive marine habitat of Fiordland is only about the size of Bluff Harbour. We now understood why the fish populations were so depleted, initially by commercial fishing, and then, when that was no longer viable, recreational overfishing by private and charter boats.

The Natural History Unit of Television New Zealand in Dunedin, under the direction of Michael Stedman, was the first to film underwater Fiordland in 1990. The documentary was titled *Mirrorworld* because of the way the recurring patterns and shapes of the forest are replicated in the forests of life under the water. It can be viewed on the *New Zealand Geographic* website.

Lance became well known for his underwater photography. With his Nikonos V underwater camera he gathered an amazing collection of slides, and was one of the first divers advocating for the establishment of marine reserves throughout Fiordland. I had the privilege of accompanying him on many of his trips, but I had no intention of doing any diving myself.

—

AS I STOOD on the deck of the *Renown* my eyes followed the path of bubbles that quietly and mysteriously broke the surface of the dark water. With relief I saw Lance appear on the surface, a massive smile breaking across his face when he removed his mask.

'What a great dive!' he called out to me. He clambered up onto the deck and handed me his formica slate with a pencil tied neatly to one side. On it was written: 'If only you could share this with me! 90ft, 1145.'

The very thought of putting my head under the water and not being able to breathe freely terrified me. And yet, after spending so much time with divers — hearing their stories, seeing their slides — and reading *Underwater Magazine* I confess I was starting to feel tempted. Eventually I decided to take the plunge (literally). The underwater world was an area I wanted to help protect, and to do that I needed to know more about it — to see it for myself and to feel the passion that divers so openly had.

—

'YOU'LL FIND THE second-hand dive suits down in the far corner — there are a few 7 mls. Call out if you need a hand.'

If I was going to go diving I needed the right gear, so here I was in a dive shop. I selected three suits that looked my size and staggered into the changing room. Well, what a soul-destroying experience. After much struggling, puffing, squeezing and rolling the skin off my knuckles I finally got one to fit. Without hesitation I bought it.

Why did it look so easy when I watched the divers gearing up on board? I was 43, quite fit and still with a reasonable figure — it really shouldn't have been so hard.

That night I proudly put it on for Lance and paraded around the living room.

'What on earth made you buy that one, Ruth? I can't believe anyone would sell you a suit that big!'

He gathered up all the surplus rolls of neoprene that had formed like waves around my waist, bust, ankles and legs. 'Honey, this will fill up with air and you'll be like a big black bubble floating on the surface!'

Undeterred, I registered for an open-water diving course run by PADI (Professional Association of Diving Instructors). My trustworthy, confident, friendly instructor, Doug Ridley (who I referred to as TCFI), gave each of us a folder full of information plus a diver's manual.

'Read the first section, and I'll see you all next week,' he said, oozing confidence.

I bought the rest of the gear I needed, with help from

Lance, though I kept the oversized dive suit, much to his dismay. All up, to completely outfit myself with mainly second-hand gear cost me just under $2000.

I was as ready as I would ever be.

—

DIVE MANUAL, PAGE 1:

> *Welcome to the course. Congratulations on your decision to pursue the excitement and adventure of diving.*

So far so good. Page 2 presented the first hurdle. Two of the five goals literally sent shivers through me:

> *Swim at least 40 feet underwater on a single breath.*

> *Dive to a depth of 8–10 feet, recover a 5 lb object, and swim the object to the surface.*

I rang TCFI immediately.

'Doug, I have a slight difficulty. I can't swim underwater and I'm scared to put my head under.'

'No problem. You have to do both to continue on the course, but don't worry, it's easy. Leave it to me.'

The more I read about this exciting, adventurous sport, the more convinced I became that diving was not for me.

On the night of our first lecture, the four of us watched slides and listened intently. I took copious notes, the one part I was good at. TCFI was so confident that we would all achieve every goal outlined in our manual that even I was beginning to think he was right.

Our first dive was organised for Lake Te Anau, 10 a.m. on Saturday. 'See you there, buddies!'

—

THE SUN WAS SHINING, the lake looked inviting and here we were, buddy checks completed. My heart rate was going through the roof and my stomach felt as if a tiny man was using it as a basketball.

The great thing about a 7-ml wetsuit is that it's very hard to sink. Even with 28 pounds of lead around my waist I remained afloat, looking like a large piece of flotsam, just as Lance had predicted.

'You seem to have a buoyancy problem,' TCFI laughed. He put a couple of large rocks into my buoyancy vest and pointed down. 'Go on, down you go. Just go down, pick up a rock and bring it up.'

I nodded, still feeling a little confident as my flippered feet were glued to the bottom. After three huge gasps of air I stuck my head under the surface, eyes clenched tightly.

Alarm bells immediately sounded in my head, my legs started to thrash the water into a foam, and my arms flapped madly. I was still in shallow water. I spat out the snorkel and swallowed some water in my panic.

TCFI was beside me, and step by step he took me through it all again. 'It's all right, Ruth, you can do this.'

I nodded. I can do this. I can do this. Here I go! With a quick breath I ducked down and grabbed a rock. I burst to the surface with the gusto of a full orchestra playing the final movement of Beethoven's Fifth Symphony. I literally blasted the snorkel clear and gasped for air. I had done it! I repeated it a number of times until TCFI gave me a nod of approval and put a tick beside my name. Goal achieved!

Now for an actual dive. I felt like a beached whale as I hobbled down to the water's edge. TCFI clearly explained what we were going to do, finishing with: 'It's easy; you can all do this.'

I placed the regulator in my mouth, ducked underwater and immediately my breathing rate doubled. Bubbles exploded around my head with such energy that I could feel them. 'Relax, Ruth,' I kept telling myself. The three others had swum off into deeper water while I was still perfecting the moves of a flounder. Sand, pebbles and small rocks flew off the bottom as my fins flapped uncontrollably in every direction. But slowly I moved to clearer water, and found TCFI had been right. I *could* do it! One by one, the small goals he set were being ticked off.

Our second dive was off the wharf in Lake Te Anau — to 30 feet. Exciting stuff! I had more confidence now but I was having trouble with my ears and also my buoyancy. To make matters worse my father-in-law, Lucky, was standing on the wharf watching proceedings with a critical eye.

I felt like an underwater bungy jumper — my depth gauge was in a frenzy as it tried to keep up with me. When I broke the surface for a third time, having failed to stay down, I looked across to Lucky with a good-natured curse.

'Having trouble with your buoyancy, Shorty?' he shouted to me.

Removing my snorkel, I yelled back, 'Why don't you just bugger off home!'

With determination I sank to the bottom again and crash-landed on the sand, my legs waving above my head as I struggled to get myself under control. Through the thick clouds of silt and sand I caught sight of TCFI, who signalled to see if I was okay. With a final thrash of fins I regained control and returned his signal. Thumbs up.

'I think a swim down the Waiau River tomorrow would be worthwhile, to build up your confidence,' said TCFI. Everyone but me thought this was a terrific idea.

The morning broke with a frost at minus 2 degrees. Mist lay across the river, the chill seeping through my wetsuit. We must be crazy, I thought to myself. No one in their right mind would pay to do this.

We all jumped in and started to float off down the river. Trout lying in the shallows nestled into the rocks, some lazily swimming away. This was great; I felt terrific.

Then came the rapids.

TCFI hung on to my hand and away we went on a rollercoaster. Oh God! Rocks whizzed past beneath me; when I dared to look up my mask was fizzing with white water.

'Don't look up, Ruth!' TCFI released my hand and I was on my own, speeding down the river. I was terrified.

Finally it was over and the noise of the river was replaced by the sound of my heart beating. I floated towards my buddy, who had been waiting for me.

'What a buzz — how bloody fantastic!' he yelled.

I managed to smile. Where exactly was that *buzz* he was talking about?

Just over an hour later we climbed out of the river, cold and tired. But even I felt a sense of achievement. Rapids? ... no trouble. Minus 2 degrees? ... who cares. 'Let's do it again,' shouted one of the guys.

That was going too far.

'I'm 43! Old enough to be your mother, buddy!' I yelled back.

—

OUR OPEN-WATER DIVES were undertaken in Milford Sound — how extravagant was that! It's one of the top tourist spots in the world and on the wishlist of most divers.

Black ice covered the roads, snow capped the mountains and the air was crisp. I was apprehensive but excited. In the water and down we went. My ears cleared easily. I relaxed and slowed my breathing down, signalled okay to my buddy. Then, looming out of the darkness cruised seven enormous shapes. I stared at them as they cut smoothly through the water. Oh no — not sharks! Please God, not sharks . . .

My eyes hurt from staring, too scared to blink. The shapes came closer until . . . *wow!* A pod of dolphins. I opened my arms, wanting to hug them, wanting to thank them. I was actually crying — it was as though they knew that one of my dreams was to see dolphins underwater. They hovered in front of us, a calf tucked under its mother, then disappeared into the darkness.

If this was diving, I was a convert!

Reality hit me when I surfaced. 'Come on, Granny, get back in the boat. We have another dive to do!' yelled my young buddy.

—

WE'D BEEN ASKED when we first started the course why we wanted to learn to dive. For me it was something special I could share with Lance, and I wanted to see dolphins, seals and whales underwater. I also wanted to overcome my fear.

On 1 June 1989 I finally went for my first dive with Lance. Eager to display my new-found skills, I pulled on my gear and did a buddy check with him. Then, like the expert diver he was, he stepped off the boat into the water. He turned and floated, facing me.

'Come on, love, it's great. Come on.'

I stood on the deck and looked at the dark, tannin-stained water, then across at him.

'Come on, you can do it!' he called. 'Jump! Just hold your mask and jump.'

I took a deep breath, closed my eyes and stepped off the boat. Lance swam across to me, took my hand and together we swam across to the rock face. He signalled to ask if I was okay. With a smile I nodded. Was this really me, the woman who until recently couldn't put her head under the water?

During the 30-minute dive at Tricky Cove in Doubtful Sound I handed him the small formica slate he had given me a couple of years before. He read it, pencilled in the date, removed his snorkel and kissed me.

TALES FROM THE BOOKSHOPS: TE ANAU'S FIRST BOOKSHOP

—

RON AND JAN PALMER wrote to me after reading *The Bookseller at the End of the World*, ordering 10 signed copies and also offering me an opportunity to go through Ron's library. They were in the process of selling their Christchurch home and moving into a retirement village. Of course the word 'downsizing' does not come close to conveying the feelings of sadness and loss that people experience when they embark on this massive undertaking.

Over time we exchanged a number of letters and emails, and many of their books made their way into my bookshops. It wasn't until Ron sent me an envelope thick with folded pages that I learnt about the first bookshop in Te Anau.

Ron and Jan came to Fiordland to live in 1968. He worked in tourism and was involved in many local issues, including the 'Save Lake Manapōuri' and 'Protect Lake Te Anau' campaigns. Ron was also involved in setting up the Fiordland volunteer ambulance service.

After Ron resigned from Fiordland Travel, he and Jan decided to open a bookshop. John Donaldson, the local pharmacist, offered a room above the pharmacy as a location, and Ron and

Jan got to work. As their confidence grew, they purchased the Takahe Coffee Bar and this became a combined coffee shop/bookshop, one of the first of these 'in vogue' establishments in New Zealand.

The business did well and they needed more space, so were delighted to win a balloted section at the northern end of the Te Anau business area. After building delays and cost increases, the shop was eventually finished and the business moved in.

Ron and Jan became agents for the *Otago Daily Times*, the Christchurch *Press* and the *Sydney Morning Herald*, and eventually the *Southland Times* joined the party. The *Press* arrived daily at 11.30 on a Mount Cook Airline flight from Christchurch to Manapōuri.

There were a few problems with magazine deliveries, and often bundles from distributors Gordon & Gotch in Dunedin would be found languishing at the Palmerston railway station. Ron had to appear at a sitting of the local licensing authority to give an assurance that the Fiordland volunteer ambulance service would not be used to carry freight — meaning, of course, his books and newspapers.

Eventually the bookshop was running smoothly, with both Ron and Jan working. At times their young daughter Mirren — who proudly announced as a 10-year-old that she could add up money — also worked behind the counter. As their business grew, stationery was added to help boost turnover.

There were glitches. Publishers A.H. & A.W. Reed had organised to send through 500 copies of Peter Beadle's book

Fiordland, to be sold at his book launch in the shop, but they mysteriously disappeared. A second batch was sent, arriving just in time for the event, which was a huge success.

The day came when the bookshop takings exceeded $100, which was big money at the time! Lindsay Sutherland, who owned the grocery store, wheeled Ron down to the bank in a wheelbarrow with the takings, and back up the main street. Lindsay's son Neil eventually bought the bookshop from Ron and Jan, and some years later it merged with Paper Plus.

Becs, who bought Paper Plus from Neil years later, is one of my best supporters. She sells my books by the hundreds and has boxes of extra stock out in the storeroom that I frequently 'borrow' when I run out.

CHAPTER
6

DOING OUR BIT TO STOP DRIFT-NETTING

Before 1989 I knew next to nothing about drift-netting — the commercial fishing practice of using enormous nets to scoop up vast catches. I certainly didn't know about the terrible effect it was having on the marine environment, wiping out whole fish stocks, not to mention killing thousands of birds, fish and mammals accidentally caught in the mesh.

I was to find out all about it when we became involved with Earthtrust.

Earthtrust, an environmental organisation based on Oahu Island in Hawai'i (and not to be confused with

Earth Trust in the UK), was founded in 1976 by Don White, an original member of Greenpeace. Focusing mainly on marine conservation, Earthtrust has been involved with a lot of high-profile actions, among them exposing, documenting and campaigning to end large-scale drift-netting on the high seas.

The practice took off in the 1950s and over time commercial drift nets became larger, their mesh size smaller. With no limits on their size, nets were commonly 50 km long.

All over the ocean, drift-nets lost at sea or abandoned accidentally or deliberately became 'ghost nets', ensnaring countless fish and marine mammals. Synthetic nets are resistant to rotting and non-biodegradable, so they continue to catch and kill marine life indefinitely.

In 1987 nets used in American waters were limited to 2.8 km. Two years later the United Nations placed a moratorium on drift-net fishing, and in 1992 the UN banned the use of nets longer than 2.5 km in all international waters.

In the late 1980s Earthtrust released and widely distributed a film called *Stripmining the Seas*, which starkly documented dolphins, sharks, turtles, seabirds and other marine species being trapped and killed in the nets. Meanwhile, Earthtrust scientists worked to pull together the world's most authoritative data on the effects of drift-netting.

The Pacific Ocean and Tasman Sea soon also came under

threat — by 1989 there were hundreds of drift-netting vessels operating in the southern seas, the practice having moved south as the northern fisheries neared collapse. Earthtrust wanted to stop a similar fate happening in southern oceans. New Zealand Prime Minister Geoffrey Palmer was one official who was listening to their message.

—

IN NOVEMBER 1989 Earthtrust director Michael Bailey arrived in Wellington to launch the first Southern Hemisphere anti-drift-net campaign. Someone from Greenpeace rang Lance, as he and I were both registered as volunteers to crew on any Greenpeace vessels. We were told they had given our names to Earthtrust, and Michael Bailey rang soon after to ask if we would help crew their vessel for the Tasman Ocean campaign.

Lance was not only an experienced diver and mariner, he was also a skilled underwater photographer. He held a New Zealand Coastal Master certificate and Marine Engineer certificate. I was a blue-water sailor, used to living on boats, and had my Commercial Launch Master's ticket. I also had nursing experience. We agreed to crew on the *Evohe*, owned by Steve Kafka and Sandra Carrod, who had been sailing around the world for five years with their three children. Steve had offered the *Evohe* to Earthtrust for the campaign, as he was fully committed to their cause.

Lance and I both took time off work and flew up to Wellington in late November. We were met by Steve and a few members of the crew, including Mike Bailey. It soon became evident that hardly any of them had boating experience, let alone ocean sailing. The only experienced sailors were Steve, Sandra, Lance and myself.

Lance and I looked through the boat and immediately spotted some issues, so we went for a walk along the wharf to discuss the situation.

'Oven isn't secured,' I remarked. 'I could just pull it out — that'll be dangerous at sea.'

'That can be fixed,' said Lance.

'There are no storm sheets or storm boards on the bunks. The double bunks up for'ard won't be safe in rough weather.'

'Noticed that. We can empty the space below the mattress and drop it down so there is no way we will fall out.'

Lance had answers for all my issues but he raised a couple of his own. 'Did you see the huge hatch cover over the saloon? You can see gaps around it so we would take on water.'

I hadn't seen this but of course it would be a major concern if we got into really bad weather.

Steve was obviously a very experienced sailor, but what about the crew?

'They're all enthusiastic and dedicated, but what can they do if the shit hits the fan?' I asked.

'But if we don't join them, the trip may not be able to

go ahead,' Lance countered. 'Let's talk to Steve and then decide.'

Steve assured us that he had never taken on water through the hatch, he was happy for Lance to secure the oven and we could do whatever we wanted to our bunk. We looked at each other, swallowed our concerns and agreed to sign up.

—

WE SAILED FROM Queens Wharf on 2 December in beautiful weather which, incredibly, held for the three weeks we were out on the ocean. We had a French chef who even made his own bread, but much to Lance's dismay there was to be no meat on the menu. I of course thrived, as I had been a vegetarian for years, but as the days passed, Lance's body, accustomed to a meat meal every day, started to close down. He became pale, his energy levels dropped and he had to push himself to stand a watch.

One of the crew, nicknamed Cosmo, was a really nice guy who had absolutely no idea how to steer a boat.

'What course are you steering, Cosmo?'

He would look at the compass and reply, '287 and a half.'

We would look at each other and laugh. Neither of us had ever heard anyone calling half a degree — no one steered that accurately.

The chef told us that when he had been on watch with Cosmo the previous night he had watched the moon go right around the wheelhouse, meaning Cosmo had completed a full circle, which was definitely not the plan ...

There was also a former US marine on board who had fought in Vietnam. He could speak a number of Asian languages and frequently monitored the marine radio, enjoying translating conversations.

Mike called Earthtrust headquarters every day to update them on progress.

'*Evohe* calling from the high seas in the Tasman. We have four-metre swells ...'

Lance and I would look at each other and smile. The swells were only 1 or perhaps 2 metres ... To us, this was perfect weather.

One night after we had stood our watch, Cosmo and the chef took over. Lance gave Cosmo the course to be held, saying, 'Just do your best.'

Very early morning we were awoken by Cosmo racing through the boat.

'All hands on deck! All hands on deck!' he yelled frantically.

We leapt out of bed and gathered in the wheelhouse.

'What's up?' asked Steve.

Cosmo pointed to a small blip on the radar. 'We have made contact!'

We were looking for drift-netters and the contact was definitely in the area we were expecting to find them, but when Lance worked out the distance from our position he muttered, 'I'm going back to bed.' We were punching into a moderate sea, doing about 3–4 knots and therefore hardly gaining on them. At this rate it would take us at least three hours to reach them.

At daylight we decided the inflatable dinghy with an outboard would make faster progress. Lance was skipper, and was joined by Mike and two others. They had hand-held radios to keep in contact with the *Evohe*. The sea was extremely sloppy so progress was slower than planned. As it became harder and harder to see the *Evohe* in the deteriorating weather, Lance decided to return.

It was then that the outboard motor cut out. The crew members' hearts sank, but Lance quickly saw that the fuel line had become disconnected. He reconnected it and they made it safely back to the *Evohe*. It had been no big deal, but to the inexperienced guys in the inflatable Lance was a hero, and the story grew with every telling.

The next day Mike went through the dive gear, outlining a scenario of putting divers over the side with film gear to get footage of the nets. Lance quickly jumped into his gear, tested his tank and camera and stood ready waiting for the others to kit up. As he watched he soon realised that once again there was little experience among them. The trial dive was full of mishaps, but at least some issues were ironed out and the dive crew were more prepared for action in future if needed.

To access the engine room you had to lift a heavy steel

door, and one day one of the crew dropped the door onto his hand. Thankfully there were no broken bones. I cleaned the wound, bandaged his hand and gave him painkillers. He went to lie on his bunk, and when I checked on him I noticed an incredibly strong smell — like something was rotten.

'What the hell is that smell?' I asked him.

With a guilty look on his face he lifted the edge of his bunk and pulled out a roll of salami. 'I couldn't face three weeks without meat,' he confessed. 'I've already eaten one roll.'

'You can't eat this — you'll get food poisoning!' I threw the rancid sausage over the side.

We never did meet up with the drift-net fleet, and no underwater footage was taken, but without the commitment, passion and courage of all Earthtrust volunteers everywhere, experienced and inexperienced, and the support of Greenpeace, drift-netting in the Tasman and Pacific oceans may not have been brought to the attention of the United Nations and subsequently banned.

Noel Brown, director of the New York office of the UN Environment Programme, paid tribute to Earthtrust in an open letter in 1992:

> *As the Regional Director of a Programme which is directly concerned with the productive capacity and environmental sustainability of the oceans, I have*

> *observed the progress of the Driftnet issue; which was brought to international prominence by Earthtrust's expeditions, research documents, and video productions of 1988–89. Despite its comparatively small size as an international organization, Earthtrust maintained credible pressure on the issue in the face of intense lobbying by driftnetting nations; building a network of concerned individuals, businesses, legislators, and others. The UN Driftnet resolution of 1989, the follow-up resolution of 1990, and the final defining resolution in November 1991 are results of Earthtrust bringing this issue before the international community; an inspirational victory showing the power of good research and effective presentation.*

Sir Geoffrey Palmer, Prime Minister of New Zealand 1989–90 and the man who co-wrote and introduced the initial drift-net moratorium resolution to the UN with New Zealand co-sponsorship, also stated that the victory would have been impossible without Earthtrust's campaign. Palmer joined Earthtrust's international advisory board after the moratorium came into effect.

We are proud to have done our little bit.

When we came ashore back in Wellington a very skinny, pale Lance went immediately ashore with Louie the Fly, a handsome, quiet, shy American crew member. Lance tucked into a huge T-bone steak, and to this day when he tells the story he claims he can still taste it and feel his energy levels instantly recovering.

TALES FROM THE BOOKSHOPS: SON OF SEAGULL REACHES OUT

—

ONE OF MY favourite books is *Jonathan Livingston Seagull* by Richard Bach; I know I mentioned this in *Bookshop Dogs*.

Kelly Burke from Australia, who writes for *The Guardian*, wrote an article about my first book, which happened to be read by a Jonathan Bach in Coupeville, Seattle. Jonathan emailed Kelly asking if he could have my contact details as he wanted to speak to me. I emailed back and asked if he was Richard Bach's son and *YES!* He was.

He wrote back to me:

> *Stories make us credible, likeable, relatable, trustworthy, valuable, and I think it fulfils a primal need that constantly asks us 'will I be ok?'. I think despite your remoteness, perhaps you've learned that connections that lead to stories that help others can make us feel like we're all going to be ok.*
>
> *As remote as you are, one of the funny things is that the internet helped me discover you.*

I happen to work for eBay, which I will argue is the largest 'bookstore' in the world. My role is making connections between our Engineering and Support teams in such a way that it leads to a better customer experience on the site. And now, knowing you, I have a connection to what may be the smallest bookstore in the world.

I like the poetry in that.

I organised a Zoom meeting with Jonathan.

Richard, his father, was a test pilot whose deep understanding of flying and flight came through clearly in *Jonathan Livingston Seagull*. If you manage to get a copy of this bestselling book, listen to Neil Diamond singing 'Be', the opening track from the movie. Unfortunately the movie flopped, and became mired in legal wrangling, so forget about the film, just listen to the amazing music as you read this beautiful novella.

CHAPTER
7

TRANSVESTITES OR FRIED RICE?

'I thought you knew better,' Lance told me over marine radio.

It was 1993 and he was away skippering the *Renown* off the Fiordland coast. We had a marine radio base at home in the kitchen, which was our only means of communication when he was at sea.

I had been asked by Les Hutchins, founder of Fiordland Travel, if Lance and I would help him bring his latest vessel from Sydney to Doubtful Sound. I had hesitated as it was a catamaran and I was a mono-hull sailor who had read horror stories about cats capsizing and not having the ability to right themselves. I was convinced this was not a class of boat I wanted to crew on. Still, part of me was tempted to give it a go.

It turned out it wasn't even a regular catamaran built for ocean passages, but still I didn't say no. Why on earth, Lance wanted to know, was I seriously thinking about flying to Sydney to relocate a suspect vessel that had been built as a spectators' craft for the America's Cup off Fremantle and then converted into a male strip venue? He was quite clear it was likely to be a nightmare trip and he wasn't having a bar of it.

'I thought you had more sense!' Lance went on. 'Well, you're going into it with your eyes open. Glad it isn't me!' I could hear the reluctance in his voice. 'Keep in touch by radio, Ruth. I'll be listening out for you.'

—

THE 26TH AMERICA'S CUP had been held in 1987. The American challenger, *Stars & Stripes 87*, was skippered by Dennis Conner, who was determined to take the cup back to the US after losing to Alan Bond's *Australia II* in 1983. Before this, the New York Yacht Club had held the cup for 132 years straight. The Australia defender in 1987 was *Kookaburra III*, sailed by Iain Murray. The Royal Perth Yacht Club was hosting, in the last series to feature 12-metre-class yachts.

I remember listening to the racing on my transistor

radio, like so many other Australians and Kiwis. Conner did take the America's Cup back, much to our dismay.

Cougar, the catamaran I was about to join in Sydney, had been built for spectators at that event, with life-jackets available for all passengers and crew, and numerous life-rafts on the upper deck.

Undeterred by Lance's caution, I flew to Sydney on Tuesday 23 March in what turned out to be the only uneventful leg of the whole adventure. I should have known.

Cougar was tied alongside at Woodleys shipyard in Berrys Bay. Les was standing on the wharf as I arrived, brow furrowed, hands deep in his pockets, leaning forward staring at the vessel. Beside him was his old school mate Russell, in dirty overalls and also looking serious, trying to look important as he yelled something to someone on board, arms waving.

Cougar sat fat and lazy at her berth, seemingly oblivious to the hive of activity around her. After a brief welcome from Les, I went on board have a look around. Everything had been stripped out except for the bar, the life-jackets and life-rafts. There were no bunks or galley. She had tiny fuel tanks so 24 huge 200-litre drums of diesel were stowed on the lower deck, each lashed to the heavy wooden cross-beams that had been erected to secure them.

On the upper deck an array of blue plastic deckchairs waited in vain for the next rush of eager passengers signed up for an evening harbour cruise, drinking and snacking while scantily clad 'boys' entertained them. But those days were over.

I knew the boat was going to be basic, but not this basic. Somehow we had to prepare *Cougar* for an ocean voyage. It seemed an impossible task.

The catamaran had been built by North Queensland Engineers and Agents, so was structurally well founded. The bridge was wide, blinking with dials, switches, electronics and music gear.

'Where's the helm?' I asked, after noticing that this rather crucial piece of equipment seemed to be missing.

'She steers with this little button,' replied Jim, who had popped up from down below. He fingered the button with apprehension — or was that just my imagination? Jim had been working for Fiordland Travel for nine years, initially as maintenance manager and then as the company engineer. He had built boats as a younger man.

A stack of mattresses still wrapped in plastic lay on the lower deck. We would be sleeping together on these among the drums of diesel or on the upper aft deck. 'Just pick a space, Ruth. There's plenty to choose from.'

Les, as usual, was in a rush to get moving. I dropped my bag on board and we headed off in a taxi with a large shopping list. Extra timber to shore up more drums of fuel, gas for cooking, various nuts and bolts for last-minute jobs, and food to keep us going until we got under way.

The taxi cost A$45 so Les decided to rent a small car at $25 a day. He laughingly told the woman behind the desk at Bayswater Rentals that I was his daughter ...

—

FOR THE NEXT few days everyone pitched in to make *Cougar* seaworthy. Our crew would be Les as skipper, Russell, Jim, Neville (a mechanic from Fiordland Travel embarking on his first ocean voyage), David (a ring-in Indian engineer off a large container ship) and myself. Neville and David were currently working on the engines. Covered in grease, they would occasionally make a brief appearance before slipping away like moles back down to the engine room.

As there was very little water storage on board, we went up to Wynyard Travelodge at the end of the first day for showers. We all scrubbed up and headed for Kings Cross, my old stamping ground as a youth/welfare officer, for dinner. The waiter — small, dapper and attentive — took our orders. Les ordered steak. 'With French fries, baked potatoes or fried rice, sir?' the waiter asked. Les looked blankly at me. 'What did he say? Did he say transvestites?' I'd never realised Les had trouble with his hearing. Or maybe seeing the working girls on the street and the boys mincing along the footpaths had blown his concentration.

'No,' I replied, 'he said *fried rice*.'

'Thank God. I was beginning to wonder what kind of place you had brought us to!'

Back on board, Les climbed into his classy shortie pyjamas, spotless white with a splatter of black hands all over them. I called them his 'hands-on-experience pyjamas'. He was sleeping against the bulkhead, Russell next to him looking very upmarket in his nightgown, and I was tucked down behind the bar.

Les dropped off to sleep straight away, snoring with his mouth open like a small bird. Russell started to whistle in an effort to stop Les's snoring.

Oh God, this is going to be a long night, I thought.

—

OUR DAYS WERE BUSY. We had planned to leave the following Saturday, ensuring we had time for sea trials after we had the compass swung. Various people came and went, leaving us with additional jobs to be done, more forms to be filled out, and further work needed to secure the numerous fuel drums.

I sat outside the rental place while Les went in to rent a small truck for the day to pick up yet more timber beams. He came out with his face crunched up like a withered potato.

'God, that must be the first time I have been stripped and robbed so openly!' he yelled. 'They have just charged me

$150 to take one small load of timber down to the boat — bloody incredible!' He continued to go on about the $150 'rip-off' for days.

Time was running short when I headed off to Customs to get the paperwork completed. I filled out the crew list and got the export number required to take *Cougar* from Australia to New Zealand. All went smoothly. Next, I was off in the small red rental to buy the last of the food needed for the Tasman crossing.

Woolworths was busy and my trolley was full. The final item on the list was suntan cream for Les. My left hand was holding on to the trolley together with the strap of my handbag. It happened so quickly and smoothly it took a few seconds for me to register — my handbag had been snatched.

I spun around but saw nothing. No one stood out. I ran to the checkout to report the theft and within a minute the store manager was with me and the supermarket doors were closed. All trolleys in the shop were checked, customers were asked to empty their bags, but nothing was found.

I felt sick — my handbag held crew members' passports and all of *Cougar*'s official paperwork.

—

AT THE POLICE STATION a young fair-haired police officer stood behind a desk looking important as the supermarket manager explained what had happened. Apparently mine was the third handbag snatched that week.

'I really need to make some urgent phone calls,' I interrupted the story. 'Is that possible please?'

'We have to take a statement first, then you can make your phone call.'

'There are passports, export papers and a bill of sale in my bag,' I pleaded. 'I need to ring Customs and the New Zealand Consulate . . .'

'Are you off a boat?'

'I can explain everything after I have made my phone calls,' I replied. 'But I have to let the officials know.'

'Do you have any identification, madam?'

I looked at him in amazement. Was he really that stupid?

'Of course I don't have any bloody identification. My handbag has just been stolen!'

The officer looked up nervously. 'A driver's licence, maybe?'

Another policeman arrived. 'Having a little trouble here, constable?'

'This lady has had her handbag stolen—'

He was interrupted by his senior colleague. 'We have other more important jobs in hand, madam. I'm afraid a stolen handbag is low priority.'

'Well, this should have high priority — there were four passports in my bag and a lot of legal paperwork.'

Suddenly it was all action. Paperwork was thrown down

on the desk, and a clipboard and pen were thrust towards me.

I quickly asked the supermarket manager to take a note down to Jim on the boat, as it was obvious I wouldn't be allowed a phone call any time soon.

The note read: *Jim, please come to the police station with the shop manager. Don't tell Les.*

'You mentioned a bill of sale for a vessel — how much was that for?' The senior policeman was now on the case.

When I told him he came to a complete standstill. 'So, not a runabout, then? Come with me.'

I was ushered into a small room where I was given a phone and phone book. I started making calls.

Then suddenly Les appeared.

I explained what had happened, breaking the news that his $500 cash was also gone.

Les just nodded and asked if I was okay.

'Can you identify this person, sir?' the young policeman asked him. 'And how long have you known her?'

'Too long!' Les exclaimed. 'Now listen, young man, I am a justice of the peace . . .'

A sharp look from the senior officer pulled that line of thought to a halt. Various forms were signed, we were assured that everything was under control and we would be kept informed. Then we left.

My bag was never recovered.

SO MUCH FOR setting sail on Saturday. On Monday we reported to the New Zealand Consulate at 9.30 a.m. with new passport photos. We paid the urgency fee and by 11 a.m. our replacement passports were nearly ready. Unfortunately, things did not go so smoothly for David, our Indian engineer. It was still Sunday in Bombay and it seemed impossible to make any progress. But we needed a six-person crew for the trip across the Tasman, and the weather was holding, so Les decided to wait an extra day in the hope David could get a new passport sorted.

On Tuesday, Jim and I went with David to the Australian Ethnic Affairs Department and explained the whole story. Yes! They said they could help. David filled out masses of paperwork and was then told that his identification form had to be witnessed by someone who had known him for a year — a lawyer or someone 'with standing in the community'.

'No problem,' I said confidently, as David and Jim looked at me blankly. 'How long have we got?'

'We close in two hours.'

I grabbed David's hand, pulled him down onto the street and headed towards the car. 'I know someone who will sign this. Just keep saying yes and we'll get this done.'

From my time working in Kings Cross I knew people 'of dubious standing' who would be happy to sign, even if they had never met David before. We were back with the paperwork signed within the two hours.

We planned to leave Sydney early the next morning, Wednesday. It was 0700 when we slipped the ropes. Although the weather pattern was great, most of us had taken seasickness medication.

TALES FROM THE BOOKSHOPS: WESTY COMES TO TOWN

—

FIVE YEARS AGO, when Westy first arrived at the bookshops, it was a slow day — thankfully! It was late afternoon and I was about to close when he pulled up in a big truck, dressed in shorts and open-necked shirt, wearing heavy work boots. I took a guess — maybe in his late 60s.

'Hello, Girl. Told I was to come and see this bookshop, so here I am.'

After we had introduced ourselves he started to look through the books, occasionally pulling one out and placing it on the counter. He was Andrew West, a wheeler-dealer in second-hand farm and earth-moving machinery from Amberley, north of Christchurch. His work took him all over New Zealand, and frequently down to Southland.

Westy was born in Hastings and grew up on a farm in Ōmakere with his two brothers.

He reminded me of Barry Crump as he chatted away, the whole time searching for books, jumping from one funny story to another. He told me he loved books and was always adding to his collection.

Westy has become a regular, although it may be many

months between visits. Sometimes he will ring to say he is on his way, other times he just pulls up and announces his presence with his big booming voice, softened by continual laughter. He is an old-school gentleman with a gentle heart.

As his finger runs along the Fiordland books he asks, ‘Have I got this one?’

‘I think you bought that one a few years ago, Westy. How many times have I told you to catalogue your books so you don’t double up?’

‘I know, but I don’t have time. I trust you to remember what I’ve bought,’ he replies with a cheeky smile.

Many of my regular collectors are the same. ‘Have I got this book, Ruth?’

Westy’s Holden Rodeo, which he bought new in 2003, has done 950,000 km. He learnt early on that selling second-hand earth-moving equipment was easier if you didn’t look too prosperous. The Rodeo gets the odd tidy-up, but is worn and rattly. In top gear it makes so much noise you can’t hold a conversation. Westy has photos of it parked at Slope Point, at the bottom of the South Island, and another at Surville Cliffs, at the top of the North Island.

I really love catching up with my regulars. They may only visit once or twice a season but we slip into an easy conversation, picking up where we left off last time. To my surprise, two of my regulars now have a database of books on their cellphones, so progress is being made. But not Westy.

He knows I have a system that allows people to return a

book they have bought if they find they already have it. Not too many books are returned.

I always give discounts to my regulars, and often I will gift them a book. Westy will not accept a gift, and always argues when I try to give him a discount — it is a ritual that forms part of our relationship. I'll make him a coffee, and while he tells yet another funny story, he secretly slips $20 under the sofa cushion. I only discover the money when I lift the cushions to vacuum under them.

Last time I emailed him. 'Westy, you have slipped me money again!'

'Wasn't me, Girl,' he replied.

CHAPTER
8

CROSSING THE TASMAN — NEVER AGAIN!

Wednesday 31 March 1993: Farewell Sydney Harbour, hello Tasman Sea.

A 10–15-knot breeze together with a small ocean swell stayed with us most of the day. David was looking a lighter shade of his usual very dark complexion, Neville felt 'off' and looked it, and as for me — I was feeling very sick after only an hour at sea, so Les took over the cooking. He roughly cut up a cabbage, opened two big tins of pears, put everything into a saucepan and boiled it.

'Main course and dessert all in one,' he said proudly as he handed the bowls of food around.

David and I were to stand watch together but I was so sick he did it alone. Within hours I was dry retching and had diarrhoea. I knew from experience it would last for about 24 hours, and after that I would be able to face whatever conditions the sea threw at us.

Near daybreak, Les woke Jim and told him he was having difficulty steering the boat. Jim rushed up on deck, and pulled back the throttle after he realised the boat was down by the head. He went up onto the foredeck and saw that we were taking on water.

Inspection revealed that some welding had failed along the starboard bow. Part of the hull plating had peeled away from the stem (the front of the bow) and was acting as a scoop. Luckily it was above the waterline, and a collision bulkhead had stopped any water getting further back into the boat.

We spent 40 minutes pumping out the for'ard compartment. Then we had to lever the aluminium plate back as close as possible to its designed shape. As we didn't have a dinghy (only life-rafts), this had to be done from the deck. Jim drilled a hole in the damaged plate and a matching one on the deck, then, using a threaded rod in a Spanish windlass arrangement, he pulled the plate back as close as possible to its original shape. It took five hours.

When I had recovered from my seasickness I stood watch with David. As an engineer on large ships, he had a lot to learn about running a smaller vessel. I kept trying to call Wellington Radio throughout our watch but there was no signal. I was starting to get concerned as our ETA in Milford was Friday and we were already running behind schedule.

I found out later that Lance had been trying to radio us but also could not get through. He was not surprised, as he had anticipated problems, but he was growing very concerned.

Jim and Neville set about trying to fix the radio problem. It seemed to be shorting out while we were transmitting, so Jim came up with the idea of holding the radio to earth it. He pulled plastic bags over his hands and told me to call Wellington Radio or Lance on the *Renown*. The whole situation was comical. David was covered in grease, steering the vessel with a button, and Jim was standing with plastic bags over his hands holding up the radio. Les and Russell were off watch and asleep during this performance.

I called and called, hoping someone somewhere would receive my message. There was nothing — total silence.

Meanwhile, it was decided that we should lay south of our course, to shield the inner side of the damaged starboard hull from the waves. Our destination was now Doubtful Sound, further south than Milford Sound. The sea was still calm, with just a breath of wind from the nor'east, but now it appeared we had further problems — clouds of grey smoke had begun trailing behind us. David and Neville set to work on the engine but couldn't locate the problem. The radar was also malfunctioning.

When Les and Russell came on deck to stand their watch, I quietly delivered the news that the radio wasn't working, the radar was on the blink, the starboard engine had been shut down and we had to change course due to a change in wind direction. Les was furious. 'You can't trust anyone to do their job properly! Shoddy workmanship!'

Russell, who knew nothing about boats, was sitting in a comfortable seat totally oblivious, thoroughly enjoying the trip.

Les fiddled with the radio, and incredibly managed to get a Pan-Pan message (a step down from a Mayday call) with our location through to Auckland Radio.

At 0600 next day I was on watch, listening for Wellington Radio, when Lance came through loud and clear. He could only hear us intermittently, so we had to pass our messages through Wellington Radio.

'Wellington Radio, Wellington Radio, this is vessel *Cougar*, vessel *Cougar*. Do you read me?'

'Vessel *Cougar*, this is Wellington Radio, you are coming in strength 1. Can you please change to another channel?'

'Negative, negative. Our only transmitting channel is 4125.' I gave them our position, and the information about the state of the boat and radio. 'Proceeding with caution, ETA Doubtful Sound to be confirmed,' I said. This was relayed to Lance, who was obviously relieved to hear from us at last.

Pretty soon Jim came up with another concern — we were burning through fuel much faster than expected. If we made Doubtful Sound we could refuel there, but would we make it that far? The sound itself was 40 km long.

I called Wellington Radio with a list of questions for Lance.

Could we get through Homeward Bound Passage (into Doubtful Sound) with our 8.5-metre beam? Alternatively, could he meet up with us at sea with 200 litres of fuel?

Positive reply to the first question; long hesitation in response to the second — but then a yes. Lance had to think carefully about the safety implications of bringing a solid steel vessel alongside an aluminium catamaran to effect the transfer of fuel. He decided it could be done.

In the early afternoon the nor'easter came up, 20 knots with a 3–4-metre swell. The movement of a multi-hull is so different from a keeler — you seem to go over each wave twice, so I was seasick again. I lay on my mattress, braced between the timber beams holding the fuel drums in place. Why did I keep doing this to myself?

At 1535 Les shook me awake. 'Change of plan, Ruth. Call Lance and see if we can get fuel from him in Preservation Inlet.'

No 'how are you feeling?' And why couldn't Les use the radio himself? I dragged myself off the mattress and headed up to the bridge. Preservation Inlet! This meant we were heading even further south to protect the starboard hull. Preservation Inlet is the most southerly of the fiords. If the weather didn't improve soon, our next stop would be Bluff or Stewart Island.

At least we could now transmit. Wellington Radio were exceptionally good, relaying messages to Lance over the next two-and-a-half days, by which time Preservation Inlet was no longer a possibility as the weather had deteriorated. Thankfully, but unbeknown to us, Murray Paterson, a marine radio operator based in Invercargill, was by now listening in. He had organised a boat that was working in Foveaux Strait to stand by, and was also scoping out a helicopter fuel drop.

—

DAVID AND I were on watch 2000 to 0100. The wind was now 25 knots, seas 4–5 metres. I slowed the boat down as we were surfing down the front of the waves, but controlling her with the blasted button was difficult as there was a time lapse in her response. Les told me we couldn't drop the revs too low or we would lose steerage, so we had to try to lay her off when a big swell came through. Our speed was around 12 knots but reached 20 knots on occasions when we were picked up by a wave. I was worried about what was happening to the starboard hull, and for the first time on an ocean passage I was very happy to be wearing a life-jacket.

Les and Russell came up onto the bridge at 0100. Laid-back Russell took the waves on like he was on a surfboard; it was all part of a great adventure. Morning seemed like days away. We had reset our course — we were now headed for Bluff. The conditions would have been excellent for a mono-hull but this was a cat, and we still had Puysegur Point and Foveaux Strait to face.

Jim calculated the fuel again and said if the good weather held we would just make Bluff.

At 0615 I notified Wellington that our ETA was 1600 Bluff Harbour.

We could hear Lance loud and clear. Murray from Invercargill called us every hour and relayed messages. Lance told me later that he was very, very worried by this stage.

—

INCREDIBLY, AS WE approached the southernmost point of Fiordland, the sea settled to a shimmering ripple and the wind dropped. We would make Bluff.

As I sat on the bow with Jim, we agreed that we would *never* do another Tasman crossing in a cat. We were so glad it was nearly over.

David was at the helm, and Les told him to stand off a couple of miles from Centre Island. Les then went below to shower and the rest of us started to clean the boat up. When

Les returned to the bridge, David was heading straight for Centre Island. A few sharp words from Les and we were back on course.

Jim notified the authorities at Bluff that we required clearance by Customs and the Ministry of Agriculture and Fisheries (MAF), and we needed somewhere to berth. The harbourmaster told us a yacht race was in progress and there was also thick fog. We just laughed. Of course there was. What else could go wrong?

The fog was so thick we could not see the shoreline. On we steamed until we spotted the harbour entrance peeping out of the murk. Luckily, two fishing boats were also heading in so we tucked in behind them and slowly made our way into the harbour, unable to see any navigation markers until we were nearly on them.

As we approached the wharf I'm sure the only thing visible to everyone on shore would have been the black smoke belching from our starboard engine. We had only five hours of fuel left when we finally tied alongside.

After we had cleared Customs, and MAF had removed all suspect food, we were permitted ashore. I grabbed my gear and jumped ashore, falling to the ground to kiss the wharf. After six days without a shower or a change of clothes I was looking forward to a long, hot bath. It would be goodbye to the mould that was growing under my wet-weather gear and the six varieties of fungus that were no doubt thriving between my toes.

Soon after this crossing, Les had another bright idea — relocating a submarine to Milford Sound to run tourist trips. Knowing my brief submarine experience, he clearly had me in mind. The question was asked. My answer? 'NO!'

To my relief, the idea slowly died.

Cougar was fully restored, renamed *Commander Peak*, and began a new career as a tourist vessel in Doubtful Sound.

TALES FROM THE BOOKSHOPS: LURED BY TROUT

—

HE WAS WEARING a wide-brimmed hat with colourful flies scattered around the band, his sunglasses were tucked into the top pocket of his fishing vest, and he wore waterproof over-trousers. The only piece of clothing that was not part of his fishing attire was the pink scarf around his neck.

He had visited my bookshops about a week before, spending about an hour looking through the fishing books as he sat comfortably tucked in the corner in The Snug.

Not wanting to disturb him, I waited until he stood up to introduce myself.

'Hi, I'm Ruth. Looks like you are serious about trout fishing. Where are you from?'

'UK. I usually go up to Scotland and fish in the rivers up there but I have heard so much about the New Zealand rivers that I thought I would try my luck over here.'

'Have you caught anything?' I asked.

'No. Maybe you can give me some suggestions on where to go, or are the best spots kept secret for the locals?'

'All I can tell you is that the water is very warm because of our hot summer, and river levels are low. Local fishermen are telling me the fish are looking thin. Not good news, I'm sad to say.'

He looked at me and sighed. 'How about a good book then?'

'Haven't you found one yet? What about *Trout Fishing: A Guide to New Zealand's South Island* by Tony Busch?'

'Got that. I bought up a pile of books on fishing in New Zealand as soon as I arrived.'

'Have you heard of Stu Tripney, a fishing guide in Athol? He makes great flies and has written a pile of books . . .'

'Checked out his books — not my thing.'

I was starting to think he didn't really want a 'how to fish' book so I took a gamble. 'Have you read *The Feather Thief: The Natural History Heist of the Century* by Kirk Wallace Johnson? It might not be a book you would normally pick up but I think you'd find it really interesting.'

'What's it about?'

'The sale of rare bird feathers on the international black market — feathers used for tying flies. Do you tie your own flies?'

'Of course.' He extracted one from his hat. 'See this one? It's a shoulder feather from a partridge.' He pulled out another. 'This one is from the wing.'

'I know nothing about trout fishing,' I said, 'but maybe our trout like Kiwi flies.'

'Wow, can you get me some kiwi feathers?'

Oops. I realised I should have said *New Zealand-made* flies. 'No, kiwi are protected birds. I meant flies made locally. Stu makes them.'

He asked about *The Feather Thief.*

'How about I lend you my copy and when you have finished you bring it back? It's about a young guy who breaks into the Natural History Museum in Tring and steals a suitcase full of rare and extinct bird specimens. He then sells their feathers for enormous amounts of money to the fly-tying community on the black market.'

'Was he caught?'

'Not telling you. I'll go and get the book.'

When I returned, he was in the main bookshop, browsing through some charts. 'Any charts of Fiordland?'

'All sold, sorry.' I handed him the book.

He turned it over and read the back. 'Okay, if I enjoy this book I'll bring you a trout,' he said with a smile.

Dropping my voice, I told him about a fishing spot close by where only a few days before another fisherman had caught a good-sized rainbow trout.

'I will only accept a trout if you catch two,' I said. 'You should have the first one.'

Three days later he returned, a small smile creasing his face.

'Got you a fish, Ruth. I caught three — great wee spot.'

'What about the book?' I asked.

'Need to buy a copy — it was great.'

He handed me the book, and then the trout wrapped in paper. 'Any chance of telling me about another good spot?'

'No, only one spot per fisherman.'

He laughed. 'Got a copy of that book for sale?'

'No again, but you can have my copy.' I handed him the book back. 'I think that is a good exchange.'

'I'll be back next year and I'll be coming to see you first, so save me a spot!'

'I'm a bookseller, not a fishing guide! Anyway, what is your name?'

'Nicholas. And please don't call me Nick.' He came towards me with his hand extended.

'I don't shake hands, I hug,' I said. 'Want a farewell hug?'

He nodded and so we hugged.

THOMAS IS A FRIEND from Bavaria in Germany who comes to live with us for three months every year. His passion is fly fishing. Within days of arriving he visits his favourite fishing spots to see if his 'super fish' are still lurking in their usual hideouts. He comes back home with a massive smile after he has renewed his relationship with them. 'I am so happy! My fish are still there!' He releases many of the fish he catches, and he brings the occasional rainbow or brown trout home as a gift for us.

Thomas has been coming to Manapōuri for nearly 10 years and has been staying with us for the last five years, becoming part of our family. He is a paramedic/firefighter who lives in the small village of Waltenhofen, near Kempten, which is by a lake, so he feels very much at home beside Lake Manapōuri.

Thomas's time with us is his rest and recuperation break from a highly stressful career. As a sensitive, gentle man, he wears his emotions openly. The time he spends on the river-banks, the hours walking through the forest and exploring the lakes and rivers in our dinghy are a time of healing and peace.

I would consider him to be an excellent fly fisherman but on one occasion a particularly stubborn fish held the upper hand.

He had noticed a large dark shape lying quietly in the shallows, slowly swaying its body, head pointing upstream. With the perfect fly, Thomas flicked his line right in front of its mouth . . . nothing. He changed the fly and tried again, perfectly landing the fly right beside the head. Again the fish showed no interest. Slightly frustrated, Thomas attached another fly.

Sitting on the riverbank nearby was his friend Hunter, who by this time was laughing. 'I think it's a log, Thomas!'

'Noooo! It is a *fish*, Hunter. I can see it clearly.'

Again and again he tempted the fish with his perfect casting. Finally he sighed in exasperation. 'There is something wrong with it, Hunter,' he said. He entered the river, reached under the 'fish' and discovered it was a small branch.

'Oh, I couldn't believe it!' he told us. 'How could I be so stupid?'

CHAPTER
9

AUNTY'S FINAL JOURNEY

I wasn't prepared to see Aunty, my mother's only sister, silently lying in her bed, looking as weightless as an albatross wing being lifted by a gentle wind.

She hadn't eaten for four days and she refused to drink.

Her pure white hair, which was once dark auburn, was receding from her forehead and covered her ears, lying like soft morning mist on the pillow. Her eyebrows were still dark, and occasionally she opened her eyes to gaze blindly up towards the ceiling. Age spots were scattered across her forehead and along the outline of her high cheekbones.

Having lost so much weight she no longer had her teeth in because they didn't fit properly. Her sunken mouth was tucked tightly in her jaw, her chin prominent. Breathing deeply under the influence of morphine, she lay quietly snoring, slow and long, then gently breathing for periods as though at peace.

Suddenly she opened her eyes and with a distressed look said, 'I want to go home to the baby in the pram. I want to go in the morning. Baby in the pram.' Aunty murmured this clearly, over and over.

We all knew she was referring to Brian, her second son, born between my cousins Ken and David. He had died a cot death.

A baby never forgotten. A scar never healed.

Aunty was ready to leave us now; it was just a matter of time.

David, with his mother's dark eyes, gentle, sincere and hurting so badly inside, stood beside her. This was his mother as he had never seen her, her hands so light they didn't crease the bedding they rested on. Ken, the overseer, slightly confused, tried to keep himself under control as he stood silently, a deep frown the only outward sign of his distress.

Uncle Ivan, Aunty's lifetime love, held her hand as they walked their final path together. What was going through his mind? I saw sadness in his eyes, his mouth strongly clamped shut, his thumb nervously twiddling. He cradled her hand in his, never taking his eyes off her.

My sister Jill was totally controlled — caring, full of love that overflowed when you needed it. She volunteered for the night shift.

We were all coping in our own way, the thought of pending death opening the door to hidden fears. The secrets Aunty held would soon be history. The questions we should have asked could no longer be answered.

How many times had her arms held me, her beautiful hands stroked my hair, smoothed away sadness, wiped away my tears? There was always a welcoming hug as she pulled me into her warm body. A lifetime of memories was lying in that hospital bed. Oh Aunty, what are you thinking? Are you still thinking?

Our Aunty, a grandmother, a mother, Uncle's lover and wife — what a profound impact she had on all our lives. I'll never forget her laughter, her loving acceptance of everything I did, her hugs and kisses. She was always forgiving, always encouraging. And a fighter, which surprised us all.

We all started talking about the past, which seems to be what everyone does when watching and waiting as a loved one dies. The laughter was wonderful, a relief. Aunty was off in her own world now. Her Christian faith had been important to her; did she sense that my mother, her sister, was waiting for her? Was her baby son Brian also there?

We recalled stories of our childhood, talking about all the places we had lived in Christchurch: Oxford Terrace, Bangor Street, Fitzgerald Avenue, our corner shop. David said he remembered the shop for the magazines. *Witchetty's Tribe*. Ken remembered the chocolate-dipped ice-creams.

Uncle denied the 'wild parties' they used to have. Jill, Ken and I clearly remember the freshly shot ducks and black swans hanging in the garage, dripping blood, but Uncle stated definitively, 'I never shot anything. Someone gave me the swan. I once ran over a duck . . .'

'What, on a bike?'

'No! I had a car. I ran it over with the car. Thought I would do the right thing and take it to Pop Benn for him to cook. But when I started to pluck it, it was full of weevils. Pop went mad.'

—

AUNTY OPENED HER EYES, gasped for air. Recently she had gone blind, possibly from a stroke. I wondered what it must be like to have your eyes wide open but see only darkness. Were memories strong enough that you could still 'see' them?

She slipped back into a muddled sleep, breathing deeply, the rattle of phlegm in her throat.

Ken told us someone had recently asked him if he had been in the Vietnam War. He sounded a little affronted, thinking he was too young. But I am a year older than him and told him I had nursed some of the navy boys when they came back from Vietnam. I think it came as a shock to him.

I told them about Vietnam Rose, a strain of venereal disease that some of the sailors picked up over there.

Aunty's pillowcase had intricately embroidered flowers along the edges, and a white lace handkerchief sat beside her cheek. Around her neck was a beautiful crucifix — I wondered who had given it to her.

Jill settled in for the night and the rest of us headed home, praying that the final chapter of Aunty's precious life would soon be over.

—

THE NEXT MORNING Uncle took me to hospital to relieve Jill. Aunty was lying asleep on her side in a fresh pink nightie. She looked comfortable, her breathing shallow. The bed linen had been changed; now the upper sheet was embroidered and the pillowcase heavily embossed.

I sang to her, some half-remembered song that brought tears to my eyes. Aunty looked with a glazed stare at the far wall. I started typing a story with one hand and holding her hand with the other. I read to her as I wrote.

'What can I say, Aunty, that will make your journey easier? That we all love you?'

I tried to sing 'Amazing Grace', one of her favourite songs, but the words failed me. So I wrote. I wrote about her final journey. My precious Aunty, could she hear the tap of the keys? Could she hear my words? Tears flowed as my heart ached. Aunty looked at me with dull eyes. I felt sure she knew I was there.

Her arm started shaking, so I held it. 'Remember when we used to go to church together, singing with our arms linked, cuddled into one another?' I asked her. I recalled her sweet smell, her warmth seeping into me, her hand gently holding mine. Neither of us could sing in tune but we gave it our best. She always looked so wonderful, her dark eyes dancing, a ray of sunshine to everyone.

My cousin David and his wife Val arrived. David's eyes were full of sadness. We have the same hair — thick, dark and wavy.

'Mum, we're here,' he said to her. 'It's David and Val. Does she hear us?' He looked at me.

We couldn't know.

'What are you thinking, David?' I asked.

'I don't know.' A huge sigh, a shrug of the shoulders as he glanced at his mother. Then he bent over to look straight at her face, deep in thought. Aunty seemed to be clinging to life with every ounce of strength she had left.

Our tears gathered, then fell, wetting cheeks, matting eyelashes.

'I remember when I was in Primer One,' said David in a half whisper. He lowered his head, hiding the tears. Val put her arm around him.

'I was one of the first day pupils at Glenmoor primary when it opened. Mum was there each day helping serve out the hot chocolate. They heated it up in big saucepans and ladled it into our cups. And we had saveloys wrapped in white bread. Mum's job was to butter the bread. We would all sit along the bench with our lunches . . .'

—

THE EVENING ARRANGEMENTS had been made. The nurses were so caring, dropping in to see us and offering any help. Aunty was turned, made comfortable and medicated in a two-hourly ritual.

'I want to go in the morning, I want to go to the baby. I want to go . . . I want to go . . .'

The effort it took her to say this over and over increased her heartbeat. I touched her chest and felt the thumping. Skipping towards what, where? This tiny marvellous pump had worked solidly for 82 years and was preparing to stop forever.

'I want to go in the morning . . .'

Just when we thought she had settled she opened her eyes again. 'I want to go in the morning. I am sorry. I am tired. I want to go in the morning. Baby in the pram.' I laid my head on her pillow, my lips touching her ear. 'Hush, Aunty, we are here. You can go, you can go. We are here to say goodbye.'

She settled, but then choked up with phlegm, her chest tight, her breathing irregular.

The air was heavy with sadness. I smelt the sweet perfume of her skin lotion mingled with a cocktail of hospital smells. The flowers in the corner stood tall and straight, a gentle reminder of the beauty of life.

If only I had been able to farewell my mother. I was living in Papua New Guinea when Mum died of cancer. Although I had come home to nurse her for a few months before she died, she had asked me to leave so she could spend her final days with my father. As she lay on the couch or sat up in bed, Mum had made my wedding dress. I was engaged to be married to Matt, a gentle and quiet Australian air traffic controller I had met in PNG. He was waiting for me.

'Go and get married, love,' Mum said. 'Matt has waited long enough.'

I taught my father how to give her injections, and how to carefully turn her frail body. We cried, we laughed.

—

I KISSED AUNTY'S small, pale ear, smelt her sweetness, felt her warmth.

Abruptly she reopened her blind eyes. 'I'm sad, I'm tired. One two three. I'm sad. I want to go in the morning.' Her grasp was tight on my fingers, and my soft words did nothing to calm her. Ken and Jill arrived, and Aunty remained distressed. There was nothing we could do to settle her.

The nurses came in silently and turned her. Blessed rest returned. She lay peacefully, her breathing ragged.

Uncle and my sister Jill arrived. We whispered, afraid we would break her sleep, shatter the fragile calm. Again Aunty opened her eyes. Her eyebrows rose when she heard our voices; there was an awareness about her.

Uncle took her hand. 'Hi, love.' Tears filled his eyes and his chin quivered.

I left for a break, free to walk out into the chilled night air, free to walk a path of my choosing. Aunty had no such choice, no options left, no turning back.

I went home to bed and just after midnight I heard voices coming from the lounge. I was confused when I saw Ken standing beside my bed.

'Mum has gone, just before midnight,' he told me. 'The time was 23.42. We were there.'

'Oh thank God.' I didn't know what else to say.

'If you want to come to the hospital, we're about to take Dad.'

I slipped out of bed and went into the kitchen. We all hugged. The tunnel we had been confined to had suddenly become a gaping hole.

A feeling of nausea saturated my body. I wanted to throw myself down into the hole and scream. I wanted my sorrow to be heard, but this was not the time. It was time for silence.

—

ON THE DAY of the funeral I went to the airport to pick up Lance, pleased that he would be with me. I felt so sad I was numb. Running on auto.

Lance looked handsome and strong; a feeling of relief settled over me. I held back the tears, bit my lip and focused on the present. How could I express my gratitude to him for coming? It meant so much to our family and me.

I had a terrible cold and felt like I needed to be in bed. I kept blowing my nose with trembling hands. Jill had arranged the flowers but the colours struggled to make the impression they were capable of; I struggled to see the beauty.

Ken and David arrived, handsome in their suits. We hugged. Uncle stood gazing into space. The rest of us talked quietly, laughed nervously, our family bond strong. We were supporting one another with love, respect and tenderness.

Zane, the undertaker, whispered that it was time to carry the casket into the church. We assembled at the rear of the hearse — David, his son Luke and me on one side; Ken, his son Chris and Jill on the other. As the casket rolled out of the vehicle we grasped the handles and took the weight. It was heavy. Thoughts raced through my mind. I could imagine Aunty sleeping inside, quiet, surrounded by satin, wearing her best clothes. The weight must have been from the casket, as she had wasted away to nothing.

I wept. My heart felt like thin ice, ready to shatter and melt away. My stomach was so knotted I felt like vomiting, and even though I was warm, a shiver went through my body.

Then I cried. I cried. I cried.

—

IT WAS MY TURN to say something.

With blind eyes and wet cheeks I faced the people who had come to wish our beloved Aunty goodbye, and spoke:

Who was it who cut up her fox fur when we wanted Davy Crockett hats? It was Aunty.

Who was it who looked after my cat when I left for overseas? Aunty.

Who was it who laughed for joy when I arrived at midnight unannounced after years of travelling? Aunty.

Who always said how beautiful I looked, even when I was wearing outrageous hippy clothes? Aunty.

Who always stood up for me when things had gone terribly wrong?

Always Aunty. Aunty stepped into our Mum's shoes after she died.

And now she has gone. I wonder when I am on board Breaksea Girl *if I can call her up on the SSB radio.* 'Breaksea Girl, Breaksea Girl *calling Aunty. Do you copy, Aunty?' Will she hear me? I am sure she will.*

—

WE ARE FLYING back to Queenstown, on our way home to Manapōuri. The plane quickly climbs above the sprawling city of Christchurch and within minutes we are above the clouds. The clouds look like Aunty's hair, soft, silky and grey, with wisps of darkness. I start to weep again. I am leaving her behind, and Christchurch for me will never be the same.

Lance squeezes my hand and looks at me. I know I am a mess, but I don't have the energy to care, or do anything about it. I just want to cry, and release the grief I feel inside.

I focus on Lance's strong hand.

TALES FROM THE BOOKSHOPS: DOLLY PARTON'S IMAGINATION LIBRARY

—

A SMALL RED BOOK arrived in a box full of children's books: it had a teddy bear on the cover wearing green corduroy overalls with a button missing. The book was *Corduroy* by Don Freeman, first published in 1968. As I checked for missing or damaged pages, food or drink stains or scribbles, I noticed a sticker on the back cover. Knox County Public Library, Knoxville, Tennessee. That rang a bell. I turned the book over and checked the front cover. How could I have missed it? In the corner it said very clearly: *Dolly Parton's Imagination Library*.

Dolly Parton is famous for much more than her extraordinarily large boobs, strong voice and vibrant personality. Inspired by the fact that her father never learnt to read, Dolly wanted to encourage reading, to foster a love of books in young people, and to bring families together by sharing books. So she started a programme whereby every pre-school child in East Tennessee would receive an age-appropriate book every month for the first five years of their life — a total of 60 books per child.

She started to mail out books in 1996. It was such a success that Dolly decided to replicate the project in all the states of America, as well as in Canada, the UK, the Republic of Ireland

and Australia. At the heart of this effort are local sponsors, who register the children and cover the costs of the books and postage.

Dolly's childhood literacy programme now gifts more than two million books each month. One in every 10 children under the age of five in the US is enrolled. As of September 2024, the Imagination Library has gifted more than *251 million books* to children.

Corduroy sat on my desk for nearly six months. I read it at least six times. It was time it went into the Children's Bookshop so others could also enjoy it.

In the book, a little girl named Lisa takes a shine to Corduroy, a small stuffed bear who lives in a department store. Her mother says no to buying him because he is missing a button on his corduroy overalls. Lisa returns the next day with her own money so she can buy Corduroy and take him home, where she sews a new button on his outfit. She tells him that she likes him the way he is, but explains he'll be more comfortable once his shoulder strap is fixed.

CHAPTER
10

STANDING WITH TREES

My whole life has been walked with trees as my companions, very much like my favourite books. I have always found myself sitting under trees, walking among trees, planting trees and fighting to protect them.

I was hopeless at maths at school, to the point that I struggled to get 14 per cent in School Certificate. Our maths and science teacher, Bill Hill, gave up on me only a few weeks into high school. He suggested that during maths classes I sit at the back of the room, tucked in a corner, and write a story. Before starting each class he would wander over and give me a subject to write about.

'How about a story about a telegraph pole today, Ruth?'

'Okay,' I would reply without hesitation. The previous week I'd had to write about the day I was born. A telegraph pole would be a doddle.

I wrote about a huge tree that had been felled, transported to a sawmill and eventually turned into a telegraph pole. As I wrote, I remember feeling sad about the fate of the magnificent tree, which stood higher than all the others. In my imagination the tree was significant, strong and unyielding.

That was the day I fell in love with trees.

Even though I chose a lively street corner for my telegraph pole to live out its life, it did not compensate for the tree's traumatic death. I was 13 and full of emotions — I cried as I wrote that story, which I have never forgotten.

—

THE FIRST TREE I tried to 'save' was in a small town in New South Wales. The gum tree was well over a hundred years old but the town council had decided to remove it. On the day it was to be felled I chained myself and my dog Jerry to the trunk in protest. That tree had witnessed the growth of the town, thousands of births and deaths, happy times and sad times, and two world wars. It was part of history.

Jerry and I received a lot of waves from passing residents. Cars tooted and people even gave us drinks and sandwiches. A small group of supporters joined us on the footpath. Then a council representative turned up.

'We don't want any trouble, Ruth. The tree is dangerous, it has to come down.'

'Who says it's dangerous?' I asked.

'An arborist.'

'Can I speak to them?'

'Nope. We're going to cut your chain and if you don't remove yourself immediately you will be arrested.'

'Why?'

'You are a public nuisance and hindering the work of a local body.'

'I have always wanted to be a public nuisance — never thought it would be so easy.'

'Have you been arrested before?' The man looked serious.

'Yes, I have, actually. In Tahiti — for vagrancy. I was let off.'

Another man turned up in a council van, carrying a large pair of bolt cutters. With no ceremony at all he cut the chain that secured Jerry and me to the tree.

'Now bugger off,' he muttered.

I remained sitting, while Jerry happily trotted over to another small tree to pee.

'We'll give you five minutes and then the police will be here.'

I didn't move. The police arrived in a vehicle flashing lights but with no siren.

I stood up to greet them. 'How do you feel about this tree being cut down?' I asked the police officer.

'Best you leave now.'

I heard the truck before it appeared. *TREE REMOVAL SPECIALISTS, No Job Too Big Or Too Small.*

'How do you feel about cutting down this wonderful old tree?' I asked the two men who were now unloading their gear.

'A tree is a tree. It's either standing up or lying down.'

I was clearly dealing with people who never questioned anything. Just did as they were told.

I left in disgust, but by now I knew I was destined to fight for trees.

In 1982, I travelled down to Tasmania to join 2500 people protesting against the flooding of an environmentally sensitive wilderness area to generate hydro-electricity. The Franklin River valley was scheduled to be a World Heritage Site and yet the authorities planned to build a dam! We won that fight, which I wrote about in my first book.

—

I HAD BEEN living overseas for 19 years. The reason for coming home to live in Manapōuri was to be with Lance. My plan was to settle down with the man I loved and live a quiet life. Little did I know I would soon be caught up in the huge campaign to stop the felling of native trees.

Lance's mother had been fighting to keep the trees for many years before I arrived in Manapōuri in 1984. Native trees were being illegally cut down right on our doorstep — along the shore of Lake Manapōuri. When the management of native forests was taken over by the newly established Department of Conservation in 1987, DOC promptly turned the responsibility for the Manapōuri foreshore forest over to the Southland District Council.

Our small community was divided. Most residents wanted the lakeside forest gone to improve their lake views; only 15 of us stood up to save the native trees. We thought we were in a good position, as the Manapōuri Foreshore Reserve Management Plan strongly supported the retention of the forest, but we had a fight on our hands, and it got incredibly nasty.

Mature trees were being felled in secret at night, smaller trees were being hacked, and two areas were deliberately set on fire. I was receiving threatening phone calls when Lance was away at sea. We had eggs thrown at our office, and then a petition was taken up by the residents who wanted the forest cleared.

On 18 October 2010 a letter to the editor appeared in the *Southland Times*, signed by 103 Manapōuri residents. In part it stated:

> *The tactics that have been imposed over the years by a minority of certain residents will not be*

> *tolerated any longer and we will not be dictated to by maverick greenies . . . We are sick and tired of looking like poor cousins of Te Anau.*

We (the 'maverick greenies') were accused of stopping progress in the town by supporting the retention of trees along the foreshore that blocked their view of the lake. Follow-up letters appeared on both sides of the argument.

Then on 1 November another letter was published. Amid a lot of incorrect information it read:

> *Ruth Dalley [my surname at the time] threatened legal action so the council brought in an independent commissioner . . . She has cost the ratepayers an additional $25,000 and when the ratepayers realise this I look forward to about 250 angry people frog-marching her out of town.*

That was pretty personal. Well, if they didn't know by now that I was a fighter, there was something wrong with them. I was rather proud of the fact that I had upset so many people over this issue. I had stood up against bigger, more dangerous opponents than the people of Manapōuri.

The Commissioner for the Environment came down on our side, extending protection to many of the foreshore trees. And yet his decision was ignored by some, and trees continued to be felled illegally.

—

THERE WAS A section on the corner beside our house that was covered in a stand of mature pine trees. The council had designated it as a reserve, but back in 1992 we learnt that the council planned to sell it for $1 to the power company Meridian for a carpark.

Remember the Joni Mitchell song 'Big Yellow Taxi', in which paradise gets paved to make way for cars? Well, here it was happening right on our doorstep.

Lance and I decided to try and buy the block of land ourselves, with the idea of felling the pines and turning the area into a native forest reserve. We engaged a lawyer to negotiate on our behalf and thankfully, after a long, drawn-out process, we succeeded. Funnily enough, we paid quite a lot more than $1, but it was ours.

Over time we replaced the pine trees with native saplings and erected a predator-proof fence around the property. Our dream of having a small forest in our back yard, right in the heart of Manapōuri, was becoming a reality. The forest was, and still is, a thorn in the side of many. As fast as they were destroying native trees along the foreshore, we were planting them in town on our own land.

In 2010 the rules of the game changed dramatically. It wasn't until trees on the private properties of residents who supported protecting the foreshore forest began to die that we realised what was going on. Trees were being poisoned on private land. The offenders even scaled a 2-metre fence when the owners of one property were away, poisoning some large beech trees. It was horrific.

Although the police became involved, and the story made the news on television and in the *Southland Times*, the perpetrators were never identified. There was even a story in the *New Zealand Listener*. We offered a reward of $10,000 for information, to no avail.

My anger had to be vented. I hatched a plan.

In my first book I mentioned a couple of books on the subject of 'monkey-wrenching': *ECODEFENSE: A Field Guide to Monkeywrenching*, edited by Dave Foreman, and *The Monkey Wrench Gang* by Edward Abbey. Monkey-wrenching is a term used to describe non-violent disobedience and sabotage as a form of protest.

I will now come clean.

Lance was away at sea, so when I carried out my plan he would not be implicated if I was caught. Two friends from Invercargill bought me spray cans of paint and delivered them to me. At 1.30 one morning I dressed in full wet-weather gear and gumboots and drove out to the Southern Scenic Route turnoff, the road into Manapōuri from SH 94. There, in large letters on the road, I sprayed the words WELCOME TO THE TOWN OF TREE KILLERS!

I repeated this right outside the main office of Real Journeys, so all the tourists could see it before boarding the boat to Doubtful Sound. I wrote the same words on the main road coming to Manapōuri from Te Anau.

Job done, I placed the empty cans in a prearranged hiding place for my friends to pick up and take back to Invercargill. I cleaned my gumboots and wet-weather gear and went to bed. My anger was vented, but of course the fight wasn't won.

I was never caught.

It's hard to believe but after 35 years of trying to get the foreshore forest protected it is still being illegally hacked away. Visitors love the quaintness and wilderness of Manapōuri, but sadly, and painfully, both are disappearing with the trees. Many of us know who the perpetrators are, but so far none have been convicted of any crime.

Paul Bensemann tells the story of the battle to save native trees brilliantly in *Fight for the Forests: The Pivotal Campaigns that Saved New Zealand's Native Forests*, which was shortlisted for an Ockham New Zealand Book Award in 2019. It looks at the huge environmental movement that developed between 1970 and 2000, successfully campaigning to stop the wanton destruction of New Zealand's native forests.

From the age of 19, Paul Bensemann considered himself to be a conservation foot soldier. He even took a job in the head office of the New Zealand Forest Service in Wellington as a spy for the Native Forests Action Council. He spent months leaking information, including plans for industrial-scale clearing of West Coast forests. In 2001–02

Bensemann helped broker a backroom deal that led to three political parties — Labour, the Alliance and the Greens — joining forces to end logging of native trees on Crown land.

This story started 65 years ago when I wrote a story about the telegraph pole on Derwent Street in Naseby.

My love of trees has never faltered.

TALES FROM THE BOOKSHOPS: *THE PHANTOM* AND DYSLEXIA

JOSHUA CONFIDENTLY CAME into the bookshop, looked around briefly and then stated very clearly, 'Hi, I am Joshua and I am dyslexic.'

I was slightly taken aback, but on reflection was impressed by his mature attitude.

'I'm Ruth. Great to meet you, Joshua. How old are you?'

'Fourteen. My mum and dad have a holiday home here. I just wondered if you had any comics?'

This was the first time I had been asked that question. The extent of my knowledge about comics comes from my childhood, when I eagerly waited for my weekly copy of *The Phantom*. I now wonder what attracted me to this muscle-bound, fictional superhero dressed in an ultra-tight-fitting outfit. Maybe it was his wolf named Devil and horse named Hero, or because he lived in Skull Cave in Africa. It was all pretty exciting stuff to a 10-year-old.

The Phantom started as a daily comic strip in 1936, appearing in newspapers worldwide. During the First World War, copies were smuggled by boat into Nazi-occupied Norway, and 'Phantom' was one of the passwords used by the Norwegian

Resistance. In Papua New Guinea, the Wahgi people of the Western Highlands painted images of the Phantom on their ceremonial war shields in the 1980s and 1990s. Art historian N.F. Karlins believes that *Phantom* comics were taken to New Guinea by US troops.

Back to Joshua, who was standing quietly waiting for my reply.

'Why do you read comics?' I asked.

'I can't read a page of words, but I can read a bubble of words in a comic.'

'Is it because you are dyslexic?'

'Yes, I like reading, and this is the best way for me.'

'Great. I don't have any comics at the moment, but from now on, if I find any, I'll save them for you.'

I wanted to know more about dyslexia and comics, and discovered that the Comic Sans font has more space between words and is excellent when used in speech balloons for anyone who has reading difficulties.

Joshua became a regular visitor, always full of smiles and incredibly polite. We talked about what he was doing at school, what was happening on the farm, and his dog.

'Ruth, I have been thinking about my dog being left at home all day when I go to school. If one year of our time is just over six years of dog time, that means every hour I have is nearly seven hours for my dog. So the time I am at school every day is 56 hours in dog time.'

'I've never thought about it that way,' I said.

'How would you feel if you were left all alone for that long?'

'Not very happy, Joshua, but our understanding of time is not the same as it is for dogs. I think maybe their time goes faster than ours.'

'I don't know but I feel really bad about leaving him. He is always so happy to see me when I come home. I wonder what he thinks about all day?'

I stood there wondering as well, but the question was left unanswered as Joshua turned to go. 'Bye, see you next time,' he said.

CHAPTER
11

UNCLE BRYAN'S ELEPHANT TESTICLE

After almost a decade of working 12 months of the year establishing and running Fiordland Ecology Holidays, in 2003 we planned to take our first decent break. The plan was for a month's holiday exploring some of South Africa's national parks. We had met Michael the year previously, when he came over from Johannesburg to join a diving trip on *Breaksea Girl*. He turned up with a small Martin travelling guitar, so Lance not only had a dive buddy, but a music buddy. After the trip Michael invited us to stay with him in Robindale, Johannesburg.

On arrival we were told to make sure we locked up the house and property every time we left the premises: lock the doors and the windows, keep the curtains drawn, lock the gate and garage and set the alarm system. All the houses in the neighbourhood were tucked behind high fences, some electrified, others with barbed wire along the top. Everyone had a security sign and many families had guard dogs.

Coming from Manapōuri, where we hardly ever locked our doors, we were now experiencing a totally different way of living. Everything revolved around safety and security.

Michael and Heather, his partner, had planned an exciting safari in their Toyota Land Cruiser. First stop was the 55,000-hectare Pilanesberg National Park, three hours' drive away. Our hosts had a deep knowledge of the local flora and fauna so they made great guides.

When you come from a country where the only native land mammals are bats, Africa's wildlife is unbelievable. Everywhere we looked there were animals — warthogs roamed close to our tent, and during the night we heard lions, hyenas and baboons close by.

After two days we headed to a lodge at Mokaikai, a privately owned reserve. Here we had our own ranger, a young man named Jean, whose wife was our cook.

It is a sad fact that increasing numbers of lions in South Africa's game reserves are getting bovine tuberculosis through eating infected buffalo. The lions at Mokaikai are disease free, and are fed live prey that is also certified as free from disease.

On a brighter note, conservation efforts over the last 25 years have seen elephants recover after the giant mammals were hunted almost to extinction. The Addo Elephant National Park, which was established in 1931 to protect the last remaining 11 elephants in the Eastern Cape, is now home to over 600 individuals.

—

MY FIRST ELEPHANT encounter was when I was nine. My Aunty Maureen was engaged to Uncle Bryan, a very handsome man whose father was Indian and his mother English. He was brought up in India and went to boarding school. At home they had servants, which seemed very exotic to us.

Every year our entire family of around 14 gathered at our grandparents' home in Christchurch to celebrate Christmas. This particular year we all settled excitedly in the massive lounge after dinner, eating chocolates as we waited for Father Christmas (aka our grandfather) to arrive.

Uncle Bryan was playing with a strange-looking ball a bit larger than a grapefruit, and unexpectedly he threw it to me. I caught it and ran my fingers over the rough outer skin, examining it closely before I threw it back. Uncle Bryan then threw it to my mother, who passed it on to Dad.

The ball kept being thrown casually around the room until it was tossed to our grandmother. She was Catholic, and extremely protective of her family.

'What is this made of, Bryan?' she asked as she handled the near-transparent yellow ball.

He laughed. 'It is a dried elephant testicle.'

Gran dropped the ball in shock. 'Holy Mother of God!'

I was fascinated and raced over to pick it up.

'Don't touch it, Ruthie!' snapped Gran.

Ignoring her, I cradled the ball carefully, then returned it to Uncle Bryan, who was still smiling. 'Is it really from an elephant?' I asked.

'Yes, it is.'

Dad laughed. 'It's a bit small for an elephant.'

As I was very much like my father — inquisitive, adventurous and bold — I next asked, 'What is a testicle?'

Gran leapt to her feet, marched across the room and glared. 'No need for this! Put it away, Bryan!' She blessed herself, nodding when she said 'Jesus, Mary and Joseph', and returned to her chair.

My dear mother whispered quietly, 'Ruthie, I'll explain when we get home.'

She didn't, so it remained a mystery for a few more years. But my Uncle Bryan had won me over. I continued to love him dearly until he died at the age of 91.

It wasn't until I got my period when I was 12 that I found out what a testicle was. Sex and the mysterious associated human body parts were hardly discussed back in the 1950s, but Mum explained to me a bit about anatomy and I finally learnt about testicles. Immediately I understood Gran's reaction that day. A dried elephant's testicle! How wonderfully scandalous!

Years later, when I subscribed to *BBC Wildlife* magazine, I read an article about elephants and there it was, in detail, all about their testicles. They are located inside the animal's body near the kidneys to keep them cool, as elephants don't have the genes to 'drop' them. This ensures they can produce healthy sperm. Although a mature elephant is very large, its testicles are small, usually weighing between 2 and 4 kilograms.

I often wondered what happened to Uncle Bryan's elephant testicle.

TALES FROM THE BOOKSHOPS: ALL MEN HAVE A WEE BAG OF SPARKLES

—

KATY, AGED AROUND FOUR, comes to the bookshop regularly with her mum. They live on a farm outside Manapōuri and the whole family are readers. This particular day Katy went straight to the Children's Bookshop as usual, leaving her mum in the main bookshop to browse the holiday reading and cookbooks. It was quiet so I went across to see what Katy was up to. Her wee Red Band gumboots sat neatly on the mat outside the tiny red door. Searching for books to take home is always a serious business for Katy.

'Hi, Katy, found a book yet?' She was standing on tiptoes to reach the top shelf. Her blonde curly hair was a mess of tangles, and her big blue eyes touched with flecks of grey glanced across at me.

'Mummy is having a baby,' she said.

'Yes, I noticed that,' I replied. 'You'll have a little brother or sister soon.'

Katy looked at me seriously, then came and sat beside me on the floor. 'Do you know how babies are made?' she whispered.

I looked at her, a multitude of answers racing through my head. Before I could say anything, Katy leant forward and said in a hushed voice, 'I know. Daddy has a wee bag of sparkles and he sprinkles them all over Mummy. That makes a baby. It's magic.'

'Wow, I never knew that,' I replied.

—

A COUPLE OF weeks after this informative conversation I was a guest at the Hawke's Bay Readers and Writers Festival. The topic for my festival session was *Bookshops Are Magic* and I had spent a lot of time thinking about how I would approach it.

In a bookshop you can imagine yourself to be an amateur ornithologist, geologist or marine biologist; research your family tree; read up on local history; lose yourself in a good holiday read — no matter what, a bookshop *is* a place of magic. The more I thought about it, the more I realised that something magical happens every day in my bookshops. Katy had given me a special magical moment, and I had to use it somehow at the upcoming event.

Only a few hours before my festival session, the All Blacks played in the Rugby World Cup final against South Africa in France. Everything seemed to go against New Zealand. They were down to 14 men after only 28 minutes of play, but the team dug deep, they were brave and determined . . . and they lost by one point. I was proud of them, but felt sad, as they had given their all. Like many other fans I also believed a late All Black try that was ruled out had in fact been in.

There was a lot of disappointment in the air, so I wanted to cheer everyone up a bit. About 150 people were seated in the auditorium for the session featuring myself and two other writers. The session was chaired by Louise Ward from Wardini Books in Hawke's Bay. The first question we were asked was 'What makes a bookshop magical?'

When it was my turn to speak, I asked the audience, 'Do the men here know that they are all carrying around a wee bag of sparkles?'

Nervous laughter, but no response.

I told them Katy's story and everyone laughed. The words 'sparkles' and 'sprinkles' were dropped into the conversation frequently throughout the rest of the session, always creating some laughs.

We all felt the magic.

Thank you, Katy.

CHAPTER
12

WHO WAS DMITRI?

We first met Dmitri from Moscow when his PA got in touch requesting information on the trips we offered on *Breaksea Girl*.

Yes, her boss could charter our boat for himself and a friend; yes, they could helicopter into Doubtful Sound to join us; yes, everything was supplied; and yes, we could organise the helicopter transfers.

Dmitri and his accountant flew into Blanket Bay near the head of Doubtful Sound, which is mainly used by fishermen as a base from which to fly out crayfish. (Blanket Bay hut, a rough-and-ready shelter that sits atop a rocky outcrop beside the helipad, is not to be confused with Blanket Bay

Lodge near Queenstown, which has an overnight tariff of around $2000.)

—

DMITRI WAS VERY rotund, with an easy smile. His accountant was much smaller, quiet and reserved. They had chartered *Breaksea Girl* for two nights so we got to know one another quite well. Dmitri was obviously very wealthy, with a finger in many different businesses, and he was clearly used to getting his own way.

When the helicopter came in to pick them up after their two days on board to fly them to Queenstown for their flight back to Moscow, he pushed his gold credit card into my hand and whispered, 'If you ever want to get away from here, use my credit card and come to Russia.' I pushed the card back into his hand, smiled and thanked him for the offer. 'I am very happy here in Fiordland,' I assured him.

A year later, Dmitri's PA contacted us again. He had decided to bring his niece, his young Russian fiancée and a close friend to Manapōuri, as he wanted them to experience a Kiwi Christmas. His plan was to fly in to Queenstown, hire a car, drive over two hours to Manapōuri and join us for a Christmas lunch. They would then drive back to Queenstown for the return flight to Moscow!

I prepared a traditional Christmas dinner, decorated

the table with candles and holly, placed the Christmas presents near the fireplace and hung a Russian flag up on the wall. Right on time, Dmitri pulled up in his rental car, clearly very happy to see us, hugging us and loading us up with gifts.

He had told us about Mila, his fiancée — how he first met her and the lengths he had gone to in order to capture her heart. She was much younger, a photographer, and had a quiet presence about her. Dmitri excitedly told us that their large wedding was all arranged, and offered to fly us over for it. We declined the invitation.

'You *have* to come to Moscow to visit us,' he said in a demanding tone. 'I will pay for everything.'

Lance and I talked it through and decided we would visit him and his family in Russia, but after the wedding, and we would pay our own way. Dmitri reluctantly agreed.

Gaining a Russian visa was complicated as we were not travelling with an organised group. We had to list everywhere we would be staying and for how long. Thankfully, Dmitri's PA supplied us with all this information.

We flew via Melbourne and the UK, stopping to visit friends, and arriving in Moscow on 17 June 2004, as stipulated on our visa. Queuing to go through Customs, we noticed a tall, stern-looking man holding up a card reading LANCE SHAW. We approached him, and without a word he grabbed our passports and pushed his way to the front of the queue. We followed, feeling extremely embarrassed. Dmitri had apparently organised this preferential treatment, just as he had arranged for our luggage to be given priority.

We followed the tall man out to the car, a new white Mercedes S500 parked in a *No Parking* area. As soon as we climbed into the back seat he handed me a cellphone. Dmitri was on the other end of the line.

'Welcome to Moscow! Anything you want, just ask me. Your driver's name is Vadim — he will be looking after you while you are here. He is bringing you to our apartment, which will take forty to forty-five minutes. The cellphone is yours. Hope you like the flowers.'

Yes, there were flowers in the car, with a card that read: 'The host is the donkey of the guest.' A drinks cabinet stocked with a variety of alcoholic and non-alcoholic beverages sat between us, the air conditioning was set at 22°C, and we each had our own television set.

Vadim was a large, strong-looking man with a shiny bald head and a deep scar running down the back of his skull. I guessed that his shoulder width was at least four stretched hands across. He was smooth and slick, and had a photo of the Mercedes as his phone screensaver.

We headed off into peak traffic, Vadim ignoring any speed limit and racing along the highway at 120–140 kph. We found out later that he had a special police pass, which came as no surprise. He even had a siren, which he used frequently to clear the road ahead of us. I sank down into my seat so no one would see me. Lance sat silently with his eyes wide open. Just who was Dmitri?

'Under no circumstances are you to leave me alone with Dmitri!' I whispered to Lance. 'We go everywhere together, okay?'

On arrival at Dmitri's apartment, Vadim dropped our suitcases off in the lift and faded out of sight. When the lift door opened, there was Dmitri with a huge smile. We met his elderly mother, who lived in an adjoining apartment, and were then handed our holiday schedule. He also gave us an envelope containing 20,000 rubles, which was ours to spend as we wanted. If we needed more money we just had to ask. At the end of the trip when we handed all the money back to him we could read the disappointment in his face.

A lavish meal had been laid out for us: swordfish, caviar, salmon, eggs, fried cabbage, sausage, salads, breads, sweet pies — and of course vodka. I was thankful that I was a vegetarian. This set the scene for our Russian holiday, which became more and more unbelievable with every day.

—

THE NEXT MORNING we visited Dmitri's office, where his accountant was delighted to see us again. Nothing was too much trouble. Then Vadim was waiting by the Mercedes, together with our private guide and interpreter, Michael, who was under strict instructions where to take us and for how long. Dmitri kept ringing him to make sure we were following the schedule.

Michael had learnt to speak English in the US and, on his return to Russia, became a translator, and head of exports for Dmitri's vodka refinery. On our way back to the office Vadim was picked up by the police — not for speeding but for an illegal turn in a one-way street, of all things! He flashed his card and the police waved him on.

For the next few days we followed Dmitri's schedule, with Vadim speeding up to around 160 or 170 kph — I was convinced he was trying to frighten me. When I asked Dmitri if he could ask Vadim to slow down, he just smiled, saying, 'No problem, don't worry.'

Dmitri had arranged for us to have a day at the Kremlin with our own guide. Security was high but we were waved through as though we were royalty. The Kremlin has been the seat of power in Russia since 1156, when Moscow was founded. Its massive walls contain four cathedrals and five palaces, along with the offices of state.

We visited the Diamond Fund in the Kremlin Armoury, which includes among its treasures the 190-carat Orlov diamond, made during the reign of Catherine the Great (1729–1796). Outside is the 183-tonne Tsar Bell, the largest in the world, which cracked during a fire in 1737, soon after it was cast. The nearby Tsar Cannon is also the biggest in the world. Its tube is 5.34 metres long and weighs 36 tonnes.

It has never been fired, as the diameter of the gun is too small for the balls, which weigh over a tonne each.

The next day we were taken to the Prioksko-Terrasny Nature Biosphere Reserve, where we stayed in a beautiful cottage with our own cook. Michael came along as guide and translator. Dmitri had organised this as he knew we were interested in natural history and the environment. The 5000-hectare reserve is 12 km from the town of Serpukhov, one of the smallest reserves of its kind in Russia and the only one in the Moscow region. It is home to over 140 bird species, more than 50 species of wild mammal, and upward of 900 plant species.

The main attraction is European bison, the largest ungulate in Europe, which until recently faced extinction. In the 1920s the number of European bison worldwide was down to 48, through hunting and habitat loss. Almost all were in zoos. Successful reintroduction programmes such as the one at Prioksko-Terrasny mean that today there are around 8600 European bison in existence, with over 6000 of them in the wild. We were privileged to spend time with the scientists who lived and worked at the reserve.

—

WHEN DMITRI WAS with us on *Breaksea Girl* he had asked me what I would like to see if I ever went to Russia and I replied, 'Bears in the wild.' I should have known he would organise this for me. After returning to Moscow from the reserve we flew business class to Petropavlovsk-Kamchatsky (City of Peter and Paul) in Kamchatka Krai. With only 11 passengers in business class, we were thoroughly spoiled during the 10-hour flight. Although it was a night flight, we had daylight the entire way. The sun partially set and then started to rise again, casting soft colours on the snow-covered mountains, sprinkling the ice floes in the rivers below us with tinsel.

We were met by an English-speaking guide and tourism business owner who was obviously under strict instructions from Dmitri to look after us. In contrast to Moscow, this city, which is surrounded by volcanoes, two of them still active, felt sad, neglected and grey. Our guide's car was a far cry from Vadim's Mercedes. There were no springs left in the seats, and the right-hand rear wheel was a small space-saver wheel which Lance noted was attached with the wrong fittings, but even so we raced along the pot-holed roads at 100 kph.

The hotel was in similar disrepair. When a lightbulb blew in our room Lance went down to the front desk to get a replacement and the woman handed him one from a large supply she had on hand. Apparently it happened all the time.

The next day we boarded an ex-army helicopter. With us were the pilot (who we nicknamed Kojak), an engineer, our guide Martina, and a cook/helper, Irina. The helicopter was packed with food, tents, a table and chairs, our luggage, and all sorts of other things to ensure our comfort while camping. We were headed south to bear country.

Apart from Kojak and his engineer, who sat up front, the rest of us sat on cushions on the deck behind them. There was no safety briefing, there were no safety straps or seat-belts. A huge crack across the front windscreen was held together with black tape. The exterior length of the helicopter body was covered in a solid sheet of thick black oil, and we also noticed that the tyres were perished.

Neither of us was happy about all this but Martina assured us that Kojak was a former army pilot and extremely experienced. When he placed his cellphone up on the dashboard we realised he was using it as his GPS. Oh well. By now we had accepted that this was the way it was going to be.

'He has survived flying in wartime and I assume he wants to stay alive himself, so we should be all right,' muttered Lance.

We landed near a small lake surrounded by snow-covered mountains. We were clearly somewhere very remote and were shocked to notice that there was rubbish strewn everywhere — cigarette butts, empty bottles, paper and plastic. After we had unpacked the gear and set up camp the helicopter left so they could attend to a problem with the engine.

'They'll be back in a few days!' Martina said casually.

We settled into the campsite, welcomed by millions of mosquitoes that descended on us in black clouds.

I had my fifty-eighth birthday at the camp. Irina had baked me a cake, Dmitri had given Martina presents for me, and we even had a bottle of wine.

And yes, we saw bears. There was 'bear sign' everywhere, but the animals themselves remained elusive so we only saw them from a distance. We were told that Kamchatka Krai has the largest brown bear population in Russia and big-game hunters regularly pay big money to shoot them in some areas. No wonder the poor animals made themselves scarce.

When the helicopter returned we flew around the mountains, landed on volcanoes, and visited the Nalychevo Nature Park, famous for its 200 hot and cold springs. Established in 1995, the 286,000-hectare park is a UNESCO World Heritage Site. We stayed in small cabins scattered throughout the mountains before flying back to Petropavlovsk-Kamchatsky.

We then flew (first class) back to Moscow, where Dmitri informed us that we were booked the next day on the overnight train to St Petersburg — first class of course!

The beautiful older-style carriage had dark green upholstery, green and gold furnishings, brass fittings, and a huge carved wooden mirror. A box of food was waiting in our cabin, containing bread, salmon, caviar, cheese, fruit, coffee, juice and cake.

I was up all night as it was daylight and I didn't want to miss anything. The small villages beside the railway line were quiet as everyone was asleep, then as morning approached I saw farmers hand-milking cows, men walking alongside the train track carrying scythes, and people collecting the green meadow grass. For our time in St Petersburg, Dmitri had of course laid on a guide, a vehicle and a translator.

—

WE HAD BY THIS TIME slightly overstayed our visa and I was worried, but Dmitri assured us he had everything under control. After four days in St Petersburg we flew back to Moscow for a day before leaving for Scotland. Vadim dropped us at the airport, clearly happy to be seeing the back of us.

We checked in and were relaxing in the departure lounge when a passport inspector approached and asked us to follow him. We told him our flight was boarding in 25 minutes but he ignored us. We were marched away, together with another man who we found out was also having his passport checked. At the border control office we were told our visas had expired. We gave the woman a letter Dmitri had given us, explaining that our flight from Kamchatka had been delayed by bad weather. We'd had our doubts about this but Dmitri had been all confidence, as usual. 'No worries, everything is good!'

A security man who thankfully spoke English told us our bags had been taken off the flight to Scotland and we were to wait. They had contacted Dmitri and he was sending Vadim back out to the airport to sort it out.

About an hour later Vadim arrived and abruptly thrust a cellphone into my hand. 'Yours, from Dmitri,' he said. I tried to ring my sister, who was scheduled to meet us at Glasgow Airport, but couldn't get through. By now we were pretty stressed. We followed Vadim around the airport as he made numerous phone calls, yelling at various airport staff while glaring at us the entire time.

Finally he took us to the Lufthansa ticketing desk. He slid a pile of banknotes through the grille — apparently a US$500 bribe for each of us, plus the cost of flights — and the next thing we knew, we were being handed tickets for flights to Aberdeen, via Frankfurt. Mission accomplished, Vadim stormed off, leaving us feeling like chastised children. We had by now concluded that Dmitri was possibly part of the Russian mafia. It was all surreal.

When we landed in Frankfurt, Lufthansa staff rang Glasgow Airport and left a message for Jill and her husband Colin, informing them that we would now be landing in Aberdeen, 250 km from Glasgow ... Jill has always said that wherever I go, there is some kind of trouble. They were waiting at Glasgow Airport when they heard their names being called over the loudspeaker. 'I knew it! I just knew there would be trouble!' Jill told me when we finally met up in Aberdeen.

When we disembarked, Lance told me to 'sit and wait! Don't move.' He went to collect our luggage and see if he could spot Jill and Colin. I obediently waited and didn't move. Fifteen minutes later I still hadn't moved but I was starting to worry. After 45 minutes I was the only person left in the large arrival lounge when two police officers approached me, both fully armed. Oh God, what now?

'Are you Ruth?' one of them asked.

'Yes.'

'Your husband is waiting for you downstairs. Come with us.'

I saw Lance, Jill and Colin, all looking extremely worried. 'Why didn't you come and find us?' asked Lance.

'You told me to sit and wait so I did.'

'Since when have you ever done as you were told?' He smiled and thanked the two police. He explained that he had not been allowed to go back upstairs to get me as it had been closed off due to a bomb scare in another UK airport.

At last we were in Scotland, our unforgettable Russian experience leaving us with many questions. Top among them was who exactly was Dmitri?

TALES FROM THE BOOKSHOPS: JONATHAN'S THIRD EYE

A YOUNG MAN stepped into my shop dressed in farming clothes — not unusual for Manapōuri. What was unusual was the black patch over his right eye. He introduced himself as Jonathan. He browsed for a while, bought a few books and drove off in his truck, with two dogs sitting quietly in the kennels on the back.

It was a few months before I saw him again. When he came back we chatted about books and farming, but neither of us mentioned his eye patch. I lent him an old book called *The Game Animals of New Zealand* by T.E. Donne, published in 1924. I knew he would enjoy it, as he was a hunter.

Come September, and I had just reopened the shops for the season. The door to the main shop was closed because it was a cold day. Tucked up with a heater on, I was working on my database when something made me look up. I couldn't work out what I was looking at, as all I could see was a customer standing on the doorstep with a very shiny light pointed at me.

Then in walked Jonathan, with a huge smile.

'No eye patch, Jonathan!' I exclaimed. 'But what is it with the bright light coming out of your eye?'

'Have a close look, Ruth,' he said, bending down in front of me. 'Come closer. What do you see?'

'Oh my God, your eye is a mirror. I can see myself upside down in your eye!'

JONATHAN HAD LOST his eye in an accident five years earlier, aged 48. He remembered the exact date and time — 30 July 2019, 11 a.m. — but he couldn't remember what happened. Over time he pieced it together from what his workmates told him.

He was working in a team of four replacing a power pole. The old transformer pole was stripped down and the new pole was ready to go in. The earth rod had been left in the hole intentionally as they had to check it before deciding whether to replace it. The power had been turned off.

Jonathan's last memory was of pulling the old pole out of the hole.

The earth rods were made of solid steel with a copper wash coating. Their purpose was to 'earth' any power emitted as a result of an electrical fault. But as the overhead crane lifted the old pole out of the ground, the earth rod broke off and flicked into Jonathan's face, right across his eye. Although he was wearing safety glasses, his eye was badly damaged.

The eye was bleeding internally, and nothing various eye surgeons did could stop it. For over three years they tried. Eventually, after numerous surgeries to save the eye, the cornea started to die. When they couldn't fix that, the decision was made that the eye could not be saved.

It was Jonathan's choice to have it removed and replaced by a glass eye. He was gutted at losing an eye, but knew he had a choice: either suck it up and get on with life, or become depressed. He chose to be positive, pushing any negative thoughts to one side.

While the ocularist was making his glass eye, Jonathan asked if she could make two — the regular one that replicated his good left eye, and another 'fun' eye. His 'fun' eye would be a mirror, and that's what he was wearing when he came to my shop. He showed me how he could just pop it in and out!

'You can have whatever you want,' he told me. 'I heard about a truck driver who drives a Kenworth and he had the Kenworth logo on his eye. I thought a mirror would be fun.'

Getting used to the glass eye took time. For about eight months he experienced mental fatigue; he was also sensitive to light and had difficulties with depth perception. He couldn't pour a cup of tea as he couldn't judge the distance.

Driving was a challenge, especially parking, and reading became difficult as the words on the page were fuzzy. As he adapted to reading with one eye, the words became clearer. Through all of this, Jonathan remained positive and slowly taught himself to adapt.

Before the accident he had had excellent vision and was a keen hunter. Jonathan was determined to teach himself to shoot again, which meant he had to go from being right-handed to left-handed, to line up with his good eye. He started with an air rifle and slowly progressed to a higher calibre, a .22 and then a .308. After two years of constant practice he found he could shoot better than before, as his right arm was stronger and the rifle was steadier.

He said it was his family and friends, and the medical teams around him, who helped him through the hard times. His attitude is that a disability is only a disability if you allow it to be.

Jonathan still loves reading, and no longer suffers from eye fatigue.

As for me, well, I have learnt a lot about monocular vision, and the power of a positive attitude.

Above Having a chat with Kahu, the injured harrier hawk who convalesced in our back yard. We clapped and cheered the first time she flew again.

Below Mending the sail on *Evohe*, the vessel we agreed to crew on as part of Earthtrust's anti-drift-net campaign in December 1989. Lance and I were two of only four crew members with sailing experience.

Above Lance the sailor — and the love of my life.

Left Me and Lance on board our beloved *Breaksea Girl*.

Left Preparing to release kiwi on Pomona Island in 2008, after it was cleared of predators over a three-year period.

Below Experienced campaigners: me and Lance enjoying a moment's rest on Pomona Island.

Above My trusty green Fiat 500, parked on the street corner to advertise our wee bookshops. Posing in the driver's seat is handsome Hank from *Bookshop Dogs*.

Below The official opening in October 2022 of the Te Anau–Manapōuri wastewater scheme. From left: my co-chair Alistair Paton-McDonald, me, deputy mayor Ebel Kremer and mayor Gary Tong. Photo by Barry Harcourt / Stuff Limited

CHAPTER
13

BEARS AT LAST

It was not the last we saw of Dmitri — or Russia. But first we headed back to South Africa in early 2006 to explore more incredible wilderness with Michael and Heather. Just a few days after our arrival I had a health scare. I was in the shower when I felt a bulky lump on the outside of my vagina. My nursing experience told me it was a prolapsed uterus, so I gently pushed it back. What else could I do? When I slipped into bed I looked across at Lance and whispered, 'This isn't a come-on, love, but could you please just feel around inside me and see what you think?'

'That's a strange thing to ask.' He looked at me. 'What's up?'

'Please just do it.'

'Am I supposed to be feeling for something?' Lance whispered.

'Does it feel all right?'

'Feels great,' he answered. 'Now what?'

'That's it. All good.'

'Really?'

I knew it wasn't, but I didn't want Lance to worry.

I took some basic precautions — I stopped lifting anything heavy, didn't run anywhere, and I did daily pelvic floor exercises. Incredibly, there was no further sign of the prolapse for about another three months, so I stopped worrying about it.

—

WITH EVERYTHING PACKED into a fully loaded bush-modified Cruiser, which carried 270 litres of fuel (180 litres in a long-range tank) and had raised rear suspension, a snorkel, running boards and two spare wheels on the back, we were ready to head off into the wilderness.

Heather had torn a tendon so was on crutches and wearing a moon boot, but this didn't seem to hold her back and she'd been in full organising mode. We had a fridge/freezer, 120 litres of water, tools, ropes, tons of food, two guitars, night lights with infra-red filters so we wouldn't disturb the animals, and a small bag each of clothing that had to cover every eventuality from -7° C to +30°. We were headed for the Kalahari Desert.

Heather and I took the Cruiser while Lance and Michael drove to Brits Airfield to pick up Michael's Lambada two-seater touring motor-glider. They were flying, we were driving; maybe not the best idea as we quickly got lost. We took turns joining Michael as passenger to fly across incredible land formations, with huge folds in the landscape looking like spinal cords. When he landed at one tiny airstrip he had fire trucks coming out to meet him, and two of the local workers wheeled out trolleys to collect the luggage, though all the luggage was in the Cruiser. At one airstrip the local police were waiting to ask Michael questions about flying over national parks and reserves.

We saw leopards, lions, cheetah, jackals, mongooses, bat-eared foxes, gemsbok, small squirrels with large fluffy tails that they held over their heads like a sunshade, eagles soaring, and even an eagle owl.

Everything was going beautifully until we neared the Namibia border, 10 days into our trip. Lance developed severe pain in his shoulder, which progressively got so bad that we decided he needed to be flown back to Johannesburg. Even with painkillers he was on the verge of vomiting. The four of us drove two hours to Twee Rivieren, where Michael had last left the Lambada. On the flight back he took an unauthorised shortcut across a remote part of Botswana — a risk he was prepared to take for Lance.

After paying a 10,000 rand deposit (over NZ$2000), Lance was admitted to hospital. I contacted our medical insurers, who reassured me they would cover all our expenses, including paying Michael for flying him back to Johannesburg.

We were dismayed when an MRI determined that Lance needed surgery, which meant two weeks' recuperation. Lance wanted a second opinion, and our insurance company did too. So Michael organised an appointment with neurosurgeon George Zwonnikoff, who it turned out had trained at the medical school in Otago!

After seeing the X-rays, Dr Zwonnikoff advised Lance to discharge himself from hospital and book into the private clinic where he worked. An operation was *not* required. He assured us there was no need to cancel the next leg of our trip, to Moscow, as with traction under anaesthetic, painkillers, physiotherapy and a neck brace, Lance's shoulder would come right.

And sure enough, it did. I was not concerned about my prolapse as I had no further trouble, so we decided to continue our trip.

NOT LONG AFTER Dmitri and Mila were married, he chartered *Breaksea Girl* again. The four of us spent three days exploring Doubtful Sound, Dmitri trying to impress his young wife, who had recently announced that she was pregnant, much to Dmitri's delight.

Dmitri desperately wanted us to visit him in Moscow for another adventure to Kamchatka and kept badgering us for possible dates. He promised we would see bears this time. The big happy man gave us both a huge hug before they left, this time flying home via several Pacific Islands, as well as Thailand.

On 1 August 2006 we were back in Moscow, Lance with his neck brace, and me only too aware of my recent prolapse scare and unable to lift any luggage. We had formed a firm friendship with Dmitri and trusted him completely. It was obvious to us that his way of life was normal in Moscow.

Dmitri was extremely happy with his beautiful wife. His businesses were doing well, but he expressed concern about what was happening to Russia under the rule of Vladimir Putin, who had been re-elected in March 2004 for a second term as president. Dmitri told us that one of his friends had recently 'disappeared', which was not uncommon for Putin's political opponents. He asked us to be very careful when speaking in front of anyone, or in his home, as he believed he was being bugged. Coming from a democratic country where we take freedom of speech for granted, we were quite taken aback.

Once again, Dmitri had planned a fantastic holiday for us. We were off back to Kamchatka with a group of his friends and family. Thirteen of us boarded the Aeroflot flight, including Dmitri's niece, his mother, and our own guide/cook/translator. We were booked into a brand-new wilderness and hunting lodge. Dmitri and his friends were going to head off on a six-day fishing trip up into Siberia.

The main lodge was finished but the other buildings were in various stages of being built. Our room was sparse but comfortable. The owner, Ramon, was clearly not happy about having our group stay, as he was not going to make money out of us. We were not interested in fishing, we didn't drink alcohol, and we didn't need his guiding services as we had our own guide.

Irina, our guide, told us that in a month's time the lodge would be full of hunters who had come to shoot bears. Ramon had a 20-year lease on the land from the government and a permit to shoot up to 20 bears a year between the months of May and October. For a Kamchatka bear, hunters would reportedly pay US$10,000–15,000. Females with cubs were supposedly protected.

I now understood why Ramon didn't like people like us, who only pay for accommodation.

On the first evening, Lance and I went for a walk down to the lake, excitedly noting bear sign everywhere. We found a rough flat-bottomed dinghy pulled up to the shoreline just down from the lodge. Although very neglected, here was our lake transport if we were allowed to use it. Ramon told Lance the outboard engine was broken and he was waiting for parts to be flown in.

'If I can fix it, can we use it while we are here at no cost?' asked Lance, always on the lookout for an opportunity.

Ramon nodded, unaware that Lance had spent most of his life keeping outboards going on the remote coasts of Fiordland and the subantarctic. If anyone could get this engine going, it was Lance. He got to work on some basic outboard first aid — checking the spark plug, the fuel supply and fuel lines — and eventually found the problem.

Lance always carries a Swiss Army knife, and it came in handy on this trip as Ramon had very few tools, meaning some of his own repairs were dangerously rough and basic. He had mistakenly ordered oversized off-road tyres for his vehicle, and when he found they wouldn't fit inside the mudguards, he removed the entire mudguard with an angle grinder. We watched in disbelief as sparks flew around his head and shoulders. He wasn't wearing any gloves, earmuffs or safety glasses.

The dinghy was soon fixed, much to Ramon's surprise. At 5.15 the next morning Lance and I set off on the lake to spot bears. We found a small shallow river and slowly motored our way up, whispering, 'Hello, bears! We are two Kiwis who don't want to hurt you!' Within only a few minutes we saw a beautiful sea eagle, and then right beside the river a small brown bear.

Quietly paddling along, we saw red salmon, hundreds of shoal fish, and then a huge grizzly bear ambling along the shoreline. He knew we were there but just ignored us as he wandered alone in the long grass. He came right down to the river's edge, then stood up and looked across at us. We reckoned he was about 2.5 metres tall and only about 20 metres away. He was magnificent. As we drifted slowly downriver he turned and disappeared up into low forest. We just sat quietly. I was tingling with excitement and hardly breathing.

When we got back, Ramon asked if we had seen any bears. 'No,' we lied. 'No bears, but we saw an eagle.' He shrugged and walked away.

Our dinghy trips continued. We often pulled the boat up onto the lake shore and walked to an area where we had previously seen bears. Wrapped in warm clothing that blended in with the surroundings, we would crouch downwind and wait. Bears sometimes came very close to us: we saw a mother with three cubs, and a large male who stood up as tall as he could to look around before walking off.

We could not believe how easy it would have been to shoot one — they were so big it would be hard to miss. When Lance told Ramon it would have been harder to shoot a running rabbit than a bear standing up in front of you, Ramon was not impressed.

Over the week we saw bears every day, sometimes up to five, but not once did we tell Ramon.

—

OUR FLIGHT BACK to Moscow was uneventful. The following day we were to fly to Alaska via London, but first we had to navigate Russian airport security, which we knew could hold unwelcome surprises. Since our last trip, Moscow Airport had been upgraded so that instead of being dark and dirty, it was now clean, modern and open.

At the check-in desk we presented our tickets.

'Have you been to America before?' we were asked.

'Yes,' we replied.

'Can I see your US visas, please.'

'We don't have any. We are from New Zealand, which is part of the visa waiver programme.'

'Do you have your old passports please?'

Why would anyone have their *old* passports with them? This was very strange.

'No.'

The official wandered off to speak to his manager. Here we go again, Lance and I were beginning to think. We'll have to pay another bribe to leave the country . . .

The officer returned. 'How long will you be in America?'

'Three weeks.' We showed him our return tickets to New Zealand.

He then pointed out another queue. 'Go over there.'

When we got to the head of that queue, another official asked to see our tickets and passports. Then he said, 'We can only check you through as far as London, as there is a terrorist scare at Heathrow.'

Of course there was.

We landed in Heathrow to find the airport in total chaos. Armed security was evident everywhere, all flights had been cancelled and people were looking frightened and frustrated. We decided this was just another travel challenge and settled down with a coffee and a newspaper. Headlines stated that 24 people had been arrested for targeting seven flights from the UK to the US and Canada. The terror plot apparently involved homemade explosives concealed in soft-drink bottles.

We stood for hours in queues, and finally at the last checkpoint, where our carry-on bags were being checked, I was told I could not take my diary with me. I didn't understand — how was a handwritten diary a security issue? I never did get an answer. The official flicked through the pages and told me I could go back out to the departure lounge and either post it back to New Zealand or on to an address in Alaska. Otherwise it would be destroyed.

I wasn't going to lose my precious diary so I raced back through the crowds of queuing passengers, waving my boarding pass at security officers as I pushed past. Thankfully the woman at the airport post office was extremely helpful and within minutes she had everything organised for me. My diary was being posted on to Anchorage. I raced back through the long queues, waving my documents, finally catching up with Lance minutes prior to boarding our flight to Chicago, en route to Alaska.

The plane taxied away from the terminal and then stopped. The engines shut down and we were told there was to be a visual inspection of the aeroplane before it could take off. That was probably one of the safest flights we had ever been on.

Chicago. We had not planned to be here but we made the most of our time. As soon as we had booked into a hotel I went down to the business centre and spent a couple of hours answering emails and letting family and friends know that we were safe and on our way to Alaska.

—

ONLY TWO MONTHS after we left Russia, Alexander Litvinenko, aged 44, a Russian defector who had once worked for the Russian Federal Security Service (FSB) and its predecessor, the KGB, died after ingesting radioactive polonium-210. He had recently taken tea with two Russians at London's Millennium Hotel. Litvinenko was a naturalised Briton after fleeing from Russia to Britain in 2000.

An official inquiry in the UK later found that there was a 'strong possibility' the killing had been carried out by two Russian agents acting on behalf of the FSB. Russia has always denied any involvement.

Russia was certainly changing — Dmitri's caution was not misplaced.

TALES FROM THE BOOKSHOPS: SHELTERBOX BOOK CLUB

EARLY ONE AFTERNOON a well-dressed middle-aged woman came into the shop. After exploring the shelves she chose a book and came to the counter. 'I have read your book and I loved it,' she told me. 'In fact I read it in two nights — couldn't put it down.' Then she hesitated before adding: 'I am part of a book club called ShelterBox. Would you consider joining us on a Zoom meeting?'

I had never heard of ShelterBox so I asked her to tell me about them.

She explained that ShelterBox is a charity registered in the UK, dedicated to assisting vulnerable people displaced by disasters by helping them rebuild their homes. The group's motivating belief is: 'Shelter is the foundation for life.'

One of the initiatives the group runs is called the ShelterBox Book Club. For a monthly payment of £10–15, members receive a copy of a selected book through the post every six weeks, and then take part in an online discussion. Part of their fee goes to ShelterBox.

'We don't just talk about the book,' she said. 'We have Q+A sessions with the authors when possible, and also discuss what families we have helped through ShelterBox.'

I agreed to join them in a Zoom meeting. Faces popped up all over my screen — readers from across the globe, including one from New Zealand. I asked why they had decided to join ShelterBox when there were so many local book groups they could join. The overall response was that they wanted to make a difference, and loved having the opportunity to do this while sharing their love of books.

The following day I received emails from a few of the members explaining further why they had joined ShelterBox. This one in particular struck me:

> *What a privilege it is to do what I enjoy most, reading, whilst at the same time donating to ShelterBox via the Book Club and discussing books with like-minded people. I look forward to reading your next book very soon and thank you for your support of ShelterBox. See you at your Bookshop one day.*

You might like to google 'ShelterBox Book Club' and check them out.

CHAPTER
14

DESIGNER VAGINA

After having a radical hysterectomy in 1986 at the age of 40, I immediately went into menopause. It is incredible how differently women experience this rite of passage. One dear aunty of mine developed claustrophobia; a friend piled on masses of weight; I think most of us have to deal with night sweats.

As for me, I cried a lot for absolutely no reason, my headaches became severe, I sweated excessively not only at night but also during the day, and I had a very dry, itchy vagina, meaning sex was of no interest to me.

Despite the fact that this is something that happens to every woman, it was not a subject you talked about. Most of us oldies struggled through menopause silently and alone. At the time of my hysterectomy I had a wonderful female doctor in Invercargill. After I told her about my symptoms she quietly said, 'Ruth, go and buy yourself a baby bath. Fill it up with warm salted water and sit in it a couple of times a day. It won't fix your headaches but it will make a lot of difference overall.'

She also advised me to visit a natural health shop and buy some black cohosh root. Native American women traditionally use black cohosh for numerous complaints, including the symptoms of menopause.

I did both these things and it worked. No hormonal medication for me. I was back on track.

How on earth did our grandmothers and great-grandmothers cope?

—

LANCE WAS AWAY at sea when my uterus prolapsed again. Caused by weakening of the muscles around the uterus, prolapse is not uncommon in women who have had a hysterectomy. It first happened to me in South Africa in 2006, and now a few years later it had happened again. I had just lifted a load of wood and immediately I felt an uncomfortable bulging between my upper thighs.

I rang the Te Anau Medical Centre and asked for an urgent appointment with a female doctor. Thankfully I had a couple of hours to sort myself out. After a shower I pushed the prolapsed uterus back inside me and decided the best thing to do might be to insert 'something' into my vagina to hold everything in place until I got to the doctor. I had no tampons in the house so I looked around for inspiration. I decided a small carrot would do the job. I scrubbed the carrot, wrapped it in clingfilm and smeared it with a little Vaseline. I inserted my homemade plug top end first, so the pointy end was facing down.

I must stress that using a carrot for this purpose is *definitely not* medically recommended, but it did the job temporarily, even though it was uncomfortable when driving.

'Just pop behind the curtain and take off your lower clothes, Ruth,' said the doctor.

Taking my clothes off was the easy part. Getting the blasted carrot out was a mission, as it had worked its way higher up into my vagina. When I finally extracted the carrot, the prolapsed uterus came down with it, sitting between my legs as before. I quickly popped the carrot into a paper bag I had brought in my handbag for the purpose and hopped up onto the bed.

'Now, let me see what's happ— *OH!* There it is! Right, we need to get you to a specialist as soon as possible,' said the doctor. 'I'll insert a ring to keep everything in place until you get there.'

I was told I mustn't run anywhere or lift anything.

Basically I just crept around with my legs clamped together, even though the doctor assured me the 'ring' would work.

I drove down to Invercargill to see the gynaecologist, a beautiful, very dainty Indian woman who explained that I needed surgery. We set a date, and arranged for me and Lance to meet with her before the operation.

I met Lance down at the Bluff wharf when *Breaksea Girl* returned from a 10-day trip down to the Auckland Islands. After the passengers had said their farewells and headed off in the bus back to Invercargill, I told Lance I was to have an operation later that week.

'Remember when I asked you to feel around inside me when we were in Johannesburg? Well, this is why. I have a blasted prolapsed uterus. We have an appointment with the surgeon in Invercargill tomorrow.'

The gynaecologist explained about the operation, and how long it would take me to recover. She told us prolapses were very common among Southland farming women, which I found interesting. Then, quite unexpectedly, she looked at Lance and said, 'Would you like small, medium or large? You have a choice.'

What?!

We were both a bit stunned. It was as if we were ordering a flat white. 'Small, medium or large, or a tulip cup?' How many men would like this golden opportunity to pick their preferred size! This was a Hollywood moment — apparently women really could have their vaginas redesigned!

Lance gathered his thoughts and tactfully replied, 'Status quo.'

The operation went well. Before I was sent home, I was told to refrain from sexual intercourse for at least six weeks. At a follow-up appointment we would discuss the situation again.

—

'TAKE OFF YOUR lower clothes, Ruth, and hop up on the bed.' I was back for the follow-up.

The doctor pulled protective gloves over her tiny hands and slipped an index finger inside me. 'Can you feel that?'

'No,' I replied, 'but my husband is bigger than your little finger.'

This raised only a small smile as she slipped off the gloves.

Lance and I sat together facing her at her desk.

'You may start to have intercourse again, but you must use a gel I am going to prescribe you, which will help with any pain. It will slightly desensitise you, Ruth, but use it for as long as you need to. And remember, no running around, no heavy lifting.'

After picking up the prescribed gel we headed back to Manapōuri.

'If it desensitises me, then surely it will be the same for you,' I said to Lance. 'Does that mean neither of us would feel anything? If so, what is the point?'

'Let's just try it out and see,' suggested Lance.

I'll leave the rest to your imagination. I do pelvic floor exercises every day, and after many years the specialist's handiwork is still in excellent condition.

TALES FROM THE BOOKSHOPS: FAYTH CUTS TO THE CHASE

SEVEN-YEAR-OLD FAYTH from Taranaki came running into the Children's Bookshop and went straight to where I have the nursery rhyme books stacked. She pulled a cushion covered in dolphins out of the bottom shelf and sat down, making herself comfortable with her skinny wee legs stretched out in front of her.

Over the holidays Fayth comes into the bookshop nearly every day, just to read nursery rhymes.

As the bookshops were quiet, I went and sat with her.

'Read me a nursery rhyme, Fayth.'

'Which one?' she asked me.

'You choose.'

She turned over the pages of the book, seriously considering each poem.

'This one,' she said after a time. 'I like this one.'

Hey Diddle Diddle, the cat and the fiddle,
The cow jumped over the moon,
The little dog laughed to see such fun
And the dish ran away with the spoon.

She laughed as she closed the book. 'Isn't that funny?'

I knew that rhyme was apparently written in 1765, so I told her it was very, very old.

'As old as my gran?'

'Oh, much older. Do you know the one about the pussy cat who ran under the chair?'

'Yes! Pussy cat, pussy cat, where have you been . . .'

'Well, that rhyme was written about a lady-in-waiting who had a cat. Her job was to look after a Queen — this was a long time ago, hundreds of years in fact. One day the cat ran away and hid under the Queen's chair, and when its tail touched the Queen's leg she got a fright and the cat ran away. The Queen was upset, so told her lady-in-waiting that she could only keep her cat in the throne room if it caught all the mice.'

Fayth looked at me and smiled, then frowned. 'What was the lady waiting for?'

Good question.

CHAPTER
15

MY OLD DAD

He sat on the outdoor wooden bench, his pipe hanging comfortably on his bottom lip. Blue eyes squinted against the morning sun, he pulled down his cheese-cutter cap as he released a small puff of smoke. His shoes were clean and shiny as he brushed them every day.

He was my father.

It was his idea to give me a small set of golf clubs for Christmas when I was 10 years old. We often played golf together around the top paddock of a farm on the hilltop just out of Naseby. It would definitely have been voted one of the roughest golf courses in New Zealand, very challenging but great fun. After a couple of years, when the number of local golfing enthusiasts had grown, they established the Naseby Golf Club, which still exists.

It was Dad's idea to build the tennis courts in Naseby, maybe because I was continually bashing the tennis ball up against the side of his butcher shop.

He was the local butcher, a part-time goldminer, a Naseby councillor, the Ice Master (who checked the thickness of the ice before a curling tournament), a romantic, a poet, and my chess, golf and cards partner. We were the best of mates, while my sister Jill was more Mum's girl.

Dad loved Central Otago, drawn to it originally when he bought a share in the Deep Lead goldmine in Matakanui. As I write this, I glance at my wedding ring, made from gold we sluiced, washed and panned during our summer holidays, a true family affair. Dad had always been eccentric. No matter what his new venture involved, our dear mum was his willing supporter.

Dad bought the old Naseby general store on Leven Street, turning part of the large back room into a small self-contained flat. The main shop was where he grew his own tobacco and brewed his homemade wine. Tobacco plants lined the shop window, where they caught the sun, tall healthy plants that he was extremely proud of. He designed and made a small press in which he could press his own tobacco leaf mixed with a little wine or a dash of spirits. The home-brewed wine was very basic, made out of either used tea bags or — Dad's favourite — pumpkins.

Along with a cat he had a pet piglet, which sat in the front seat of his small car. When it grew too big for the car, Dad had the pig put down. Why he didn't try to find another home for it I don't know. He cured the black and grey skin and laid it on the floor beside his bed, the wee black tail sticking straight up like a small antenna.

Shortly after losing his cat, Dad decided to move into a council retirement flat in Ranfurly. Like so many of the other residents, he had the beginnings of dementia. Jill would drive 90 minutes from Cromwell to see him on a regular basis, whereas I only made the five-hour trip from Manapōuri every few months. As the dementia took hold, each visit was very different. At times when he was clear-headed he would make me a cup of tea and we would play cards. Other times he didn't recognise me, but incredibly, he could still play an excellent hand of euchre.

One day I knocked on the door of his small flat and called out his name. Nothing. I looked through the window and could see his feet on the end of the bed — he was having his daily nap. I ran around the back of the building and tapped on his bedroom window.

'Dad! Dad! It's Ruth. Open the door for me.'

He stood up, looked at me through the window and wandered into the lounge. I ran the distance around the back of the flats and along the front to his door, arriving just as he was closing it again.

'Dad! Open the door.'

I leant across and looked through the window. He was back in his bedroom!

Nothing for it but to keep bashing on the door. At last he came back and opened it.

'What are you doing here?' he asked grumpily.

'I've come to see you. Are you going to let me in?'

'No! You've seen me now, so you can go.' He closed the door and left me standing on the step.

This had happened before so I drove into town, sat and had a coffee in the local café and then went back out to the flats.

Dad was in the lounge and the door was open.

'Hi, Dad,' I said. 'I've come to see you.'

He looked at me blankly. 'Gidday, Uncle Ivan.'

I didn't mind being called Uncle Ivan as he had been Dad's best friend. We sat and played cards, had a cup of tea and talked nonsense for an hour.

WHEN HIS DEMENTIA had progressed to the stage where he really couldn't look after himself, Jill and I discussed what to do. We should have known that Dad would already have it sorted.

Jill's phone rang very early one morning. It was the night nurse from Ranfurly Hospital's aged-care unit.

'Your father has turned up here with his suitcase and

wants a bed,' she told Jill. 'He says he's ready to move in!'

Jill rang me and brought me up to speed on Dad's latest adventure. 'What shall we do?' she asked.

We decided the move to the hospital was probably a good idea, but we would keep his flat for a few weeks in case he changed his mind.

Dad seemed to think everything at the aged-care unit was free. He was even given a bit of spending money each week and had the daily newspaper delivered. Other than making it known loudly and often that all the other residents were *much too old*, he was having a grand time.

We went to the hospital for their Christmas celebrations but under no circumstances was Dad going to join in the festivities. He determinedly stayed in his room, firmly sitting in his chair, cap on, head down.

Father Christmas came to his room. 'Happy Christmas, Arthur!' he sang as he entered.

Dad looked up, stared at Father Christmas and muttered, 'No need to get dressed up in that silly outfit.'

And that was Christmas.

FROM RANFURLY WE eventually had to have him transferred to the dementia ward at the Rowena Jackson Retirement Village in Invercargill, as he was starting to wander off and get lost. I could drive to Invercargill from

Manapōuri in less than two hours, so I could visit him on a regular basis.

Dad settled in really well. The nursing staff were great at handling residents who roamed all over the place, climbed into the wrong beds, and fell asleep wherever they liked.

Lance and I had organised to go on a trip to Canada and Alaska but I was concerned, as Dad was reported to be no longer eating his favourite custard squares. This was a bad sign. He was just lying on his bed staring at the ceiling.

We drove down to see him. I sat holding his hand, taking in the age spots and wrinkles, looking into his deep blue eyes, which were full of sadness. I could tell he no longer wanted to be here. He wanted to be with Mum. I continued to chat about anything and everything; there was no response but I prattled on anyway. I told him about the holiday Lance and I had planned and said we would be away for nearly a month. No response.

When a nurse came in I asked if she thought we should cancel our holiday.

Dad looked across at me and said clearly, 'You go, girl. You go.'

'There's your answer,' said the nurse.

DAD PASSED AWAY on 16 June 2010, eight days after we left New Zealand. We were in the small Canadian town of

Nelson when I received an email from a nurse at Rowena Jackson telling me the sad news. I rang and spoke to the nurse who had sat with him at the end as he drifted away. Yes, they would put his cheese-cutter cap on his head and of course he would be wearing his best shoes.

I rang the funeral home. Dad would be cremated and they would hold his ashes for us until we returned from overseas.

I felt hollow. I'd been overseas when my mother died, and now I'd done it again. I felt wracked with guilt. I should have stayed.

Lance reminded me of Dad's final words to me. 'You go, girl. You go.'

We did what he asked. There was to be no fuss.

—

ABOUT A MONTH after we got home we organised a family get-together out at the cemetery in Christchurch where Mum was buried, so we could place Dad's ashes with her. He had written in his will that there was to be no funeral service; he was to be cremated and placed beside Mum out at Ruru Lawn Cemetery in Linwood. 'Just throw a few dollars on the bar at the Ancient Briton in Naseby and give everyone a shout,' he'd told us.

The sexton had prepared a small hole into which we carefully placed Dad's ashes, then poured a bottle of Stone's

Green Ginger Wine over him — his favourite. When Mum was buried, Dad had engraved on the gravestone: 'Ours was the greatest.'

He was back at last with Fred, our mother, the love of his life.

TALES FROM THE BOOKSHOPS: LEARNING FROM SPARROWS

—

'DO YOU HAVE any books on birds?' The young lady stood in front of me, making direct eye contact and looking very confident. Her blonde hair was pulled back into a ponytail, her baggy trousers and loose top suited her. There was a small bird tattoo at the base of her thumb, and when she turned I noticed another near her ear.

'Two shelves of bird books over there,' I replied, pointing.

'Great.' She went over to the shelves, pulled up the chair and sat down with a pile of books balanced on her knees.

'No,' she said as she put the books one by one back on the shelf. I watched carefully, surprised at how quickly she went through them — she must have been looking for exactly the right book.

'What exactly are you looking for?' I asked.

'A book on sparrows. I love sparrows so much I have one on my hand.' She came over and showed me the tattoo. 'She is a female. The male is behind my ear.'

I now understood why none of my books suited — they were all on New Zealand native species.

'We love sparrows as well,' I told her. 'We feed them every

morning — sometimes up to a hundred come to be fed. They never seem to fight over the food, not like silvereyes or tūī. Have you read *Timmy*?' I asked her. 'It's a true story about a baby sparrow the author found and raised as a pet. He lived for seven years.'

'Sounds exactly what I want. Do you have a copy?' she asked.

'Give me a minute, I have a copy in my library.' I ran inside and found the small green book easily as it is one of my favourites. It was written by Clare Kipps and published in England in 1962. I wouldn't give this book away but at least I could show her and maybe lend it to her.

Then I remembered I had another of Clare Kipps' books, *Sold for a Farthing* — her first book, published in 1953. Both books are small hardbacks of under 80 pages.

I took them out to the bookshop.

'I think you'd love both of these books. I am willing to sell *Sold for a Farthing*. I don't want to sell *Timmy*, but you can borrow it if you like.'

'I have never heard of these books. What is *Sold for a Farthing* about?'

'Clare Kipps was an air-raid warden in London during the Second World War. One day when she went home there was a tiny day-old sparrow on her doorstep, with a damaged wing. She named him Clarence, and he was a predecessor to Timmy. Clarence became so tame that Clare was able to take him on her rounds in London's East End. He also lived for several years. You'll love the story because it is true.'

'I'll take it — how wonderful!'

She also wanted to borrow *Timmy*. I opened it at the page that was bookmarked and saw a photograph I remembered well. It was of the chief priest from the 'Sparrow House' Zenshoji Temple in Kobe, Japan. A Japanese journalist is buying two gourd-shaped bird houses from the priest, to house Timmy the sparrow.

Two days later my book was returned by one very happy reader. 'Timmy never used the gourds!' she exclaimed.

I smiled. 'Would you move out of your favourite warm coat cuff into a cold gourd?'

WE FEED OUR flock of sparrows every day. Humans could learn so much about tolerance and community spirit from these little birds. They are so cheeky and courageous.

Two seasons ago we noticed that one had a badly deformed beak. We took photos and sent them to an ornithologist, who told us that beak deformities are becoming more common, caused by a variety of factors, including contaminants, nutritional deficiencies, disease, parasites, blunt trauma and genetic abnormalities. I'm sorry to say our wee sparrow didn't survive, as he had trouble feeding himself.

On another occasion a male sparrow flew into a closed window, then settled quietly on the grass for a time to recover. When I first saw it I thought it was a large leaf, but then it moved and I saw it was a sparrow. When Lance went out later to see if he was recovering, the bird hopped over into the sunshine and tucked himself down beside a stepping stone. Within minutes, a group of sparrows had gathered around him, all perched on the stone wall above. They were clearly concerned, their little heads bowed as they watched over him. One flew down beside him and I wondered what was said between them. After a few minutes he flew away, together with his support team.

CHAPTER
16

DOWN TO THE SUBANTARCTIC

Over the 16 years we owned and operated Fiordland Ecology Holidays, Lance sailed *Breaksea Girl* down to the subantarctic islands 29 times. She was an excellent sea boat, a 65-foot (20-metre) buckeye ketch, and could sail just as well as she motored.

The subantarctic islands, listed by UNESCO as a World Heritage Site, are made up of the Snares Islands, Bounty Islands, Antipodes Islands, Auckland Islands and Campbell Island.

On his second trip down to the Auckland Islands with a group of passengers, Lance witnessed a small cruise ship disgorge its passengers at Port Ross, preparing to view the incredible wildlife and precious rare plants on Enderby Island. Although visitor numbers were restricted, Lance felt strongly that we should not offer tourist trips to these very special southern islands. This should not be a tourist destination. From then on, Fiordland Ecology Holidays trips to the Auckland Islands only carried researchers, conservation staff, scientists, occasional media teams and fare-paying volunteers.

My first trip down to the Snares Islands/Tini Heke was as crew on the *Renown*, skippered by Lance. This tiny group of uninhabited islands lies about 100 km south-west of Stewart Island/Rakiura and is a nature reserve. Thankfully, introduced land mammals never made it to the Snares, making it one of the most pristine areas for wildlife in New Zealand.

The eastern islands are notable for high numbers of Snares crested penguins, southern Buller's mollymawks, sooty shearwaters, mottled petrels and common diving petrels, as well as the Snares Island snipe. The Western Chain also has colonies of Snares crested penguins, three species of albatross and the endemic Snares Island tomtit, which can also be found on most of the islands. North East Island is forested and is the world's foremost breeding area for sooty shearwaters (tītī or muttonbirds), with up to three million birds present during breeding season.

On that first trip I was involved in helping with leg-banding albatross chicks and recording how the breeding season was progressing. Although it was very windy and often raining I loved the work, feeling privileged to be allowed to visit and assist on these special islands.

—

MY FIRST TRIP to the Auckland Islands was as cook/crew in 1996. That trip was memorable for a number of reasons, chief among them being that I was seriously seasick for the entire 36 hours. In the cabin beside me was Peter from DOC, who wasn't seasick but had something far worse — urinary bladder paralysis. We discovered that our extensive first-aid kit did not contain a catheter. It had all the wherewithal to carry out minor surgery, it had plenty of antibiotics for seal bites, as well as a body bag in case someone died, but nothing to help poor Peter.

When we finally arrived at Port Ross, Peter and I heard the welcome sound of Lance setting the anchor. Peter was out of his bunk and straight into the head (toilet). We all heard his cry of relief, and in response we cheered.

That night as I was lying in our bunk I heard Lance walking around on deck above me. It was calm and quiet, but then the silence was broken by a massive farting sound. How could one man pass so much wind? It sounded like he was trying to play a tune! When he finally came down to bed I had to say something. 'Your farting was rather incredible. Were you trying to play your favourite song?'

Lance laughed. 'I wasn't farting. It was whale sound — they were all around the boat.'

'Why didn't you come and tell me? I would love to have seen them!'

The next day, sure enough, we were surrounded by southern right whales. A few had calves that still carried wrinkles called foetal folds, which slowly fade in the weeks after birth. One mother came straight towards the side of *Breaksea Girl*, her small calf swimming a little behind her. She dived under the boat and came up on the other side, but the poor calf swam straight into the side of the boat, banging its head on the hull. The mother dived back under the boat to join her calf and accompanied it safely around the bow to the other side.

—

THE REASON FOR this trip was DOC's plan to eradicate feral pigs from the Auckland Islands. The pigs had been introduced to the uninhabited islands in 1807 as a source of food for shipwrecked or stranded sealers, whalers and sailors. More pigs followed in 1840, 1842 and the 1890s. We were carrying out an initial feasibility study that involved collecting the stomachs of pigs to find out what they were eating. One of our smaller freezers was filled up entirely with pig stomachs that we took back to the mainland.

As the cook on board I planned roast pork for dinner one night, which seemed fitting, so I asked one of the DOC boys to bring me back some meat. When it arrived, it smelt slightly salty but felt and looked edible. I removed the skin, which was full of short hairs, then cooked the meat slowly, basting it frequently as it had no fat.

Roast vegetables accompanied the Auckland Island roast pork with apple sauce and gravy. It looked wonderful, but it quickly became apparent that the meat was so tough it was inedible. It also tasted like seaweed (which was one of the plants the pigs ate).

Not to be defeated, the next night I cut the roast meat up into very small pieces, marinated them in lemon, vinegar and honey, and then turned them into a massive pot of sweet and sour pork.

The sauce was wonderful, but the meat was still inedible!

—

ALTHOUGH IT WAS the middle of winter the weather was relatively warm, so I found an opportunity to go ashore and explore. I climbed the small hill on the western side of Sandy Bay to watch the albatrosses and southern giant petrels in flight. The petrels grow to the size of small albatrosses, with a wingspan up to 205 cm. I lay down and closed my eyes, listening to the wind sifting through their wing feathers as they soared low over me. I had never realised a giant bird could make so much noise while flying.

They would land just across from me, walk behind my head, saunter slowly past me, then open their magnificent wings to soar off in a beautiful arc, circling around to land beside me, again and again. It was so magical that I thought, 'If I die right now I will be happy.' It is a memory I will always carry with me.

—

WE WERE DOWN there for 10 days, by which time I had my sea legs, so the return voyage back to Bluff was just another ocean passage.

Lance called up Murray Paterson, who had helped us on our Tasman crossing, for a weather report. Murray operated ZLTH marine radio station out of Invercargill. He'd been an engineer before he had a serious accident that left him quadriplegic. He had slight movement only of his head, shoulders and right arm, so his radio set was customised for him. His right wrist was encased in a leather brace that allowed him to control the special microphone switch. All the other buttons and switches had been replaced by toggles so he could control them with a flick of his hand.

Whenever Murray's breathing went into spasm, his wife Faye would stand behind him and continually squeeze him so he had enough air to talk on the radio. He read marine forecasts three or four times a day, helped repair engines over the radio, and organised anything skippers requested. As I had a marine radio at home and in the office I could always keep in touch with Lance, but it was Murray who kept me sane when I knew Lance was out in horrendous Southern Ocean weather conditions.

There were no marine weather forecasts for the subantarctic, Foveaux Strait being the southernmost sea covered. Lance relied on Murray, who was better than any official marine forecaster.

'ZLTH, ZLTH. This is ZMBG *Breaksea Girl*, do you copy, Murray?'

'Copy, Lance, how is your weather?'

'If you are not too busy, why don't you tell me what I have now.'

'Stand by.'

Then within 10–15 minutes Murray would call back with a description of the current weather and sea state. He was nearly always correct. Lance considered Murray a hero, as he had bailed out many southern-water skippers with an accurate diagnosis of mechanical problems and how to fix them — without laying eyes on the faulty equipment in question.

When Murray died, his funeral was held in the First Church on Tay Street, Invercargill. Lance was at sea so I attended the service, together with skippers, crews and families from nearly all the boats working the southern and Fiordland waters. At the end of the service the skippers stood up one at a time, each giving their call sign and the name of their vessel. I was in tears when I stood up on behalf of Lance and *Breaksea Girl*.

'ZLTH, ZLTH. This is ZMBG *Breaksea Girl* calling. Over and out.'

TALES FROM THE BOOKSHOPS: LIGHTHOUSES AT THE END OF THE WORLD

—

I HAVE ALWAYS loved lighthouses. In my first book I discussed a number of books about lighthouses, and mentioned that between 1790 and 1940, eight members of the family of Robert Louis Stevenson (author of *Treasure Island* and *Kidnapped*) planned, designed and constructed the 97 manned lighthouses that still stand around the Scottish coast.

Before I wrote that book, Lance's son Dane had a lighthouse tattooed on his upper arm. A love of lighthouses seems to run in our family.

Around Mother's Day 2024, Lance and I visited Melbourne to have some precious time with Dane, his wife Phil and our grandchildren. A beautiful bunch of subtle pink, sweet-smelling roses sat on the bedside table of our room, together with a present. I waited until I was tucked up in the cosy bed before I slowly opened the gift, which I had guessed was a book — of course.

'Lance! Look at the book Dane has bought me!'

Lance glanced up from his own book to gaze at the beautiful hard-covered book I was holding.

'Wow, you'll love that,' he said with growing interest.

I read the title out loud: '*A Brief Atlas of the Lighthouses at the End of the World*, by González Macías, a Spanish writer, graphic designer and publisher. How brilliant — it could be a companion to *The Bookseller at the End of the World*!'

The opening pages had a quote from Jules Verne's novel *The Lighthouse at the End of the World* (1901):

> *Needless to say, the Lighthouse at the End of the World had a fixed light, and there was no fear that the captain of a ship might confuse it with some other, since no other lighthouse existed around these parts.*

The lighthouse Verne was writing about is located 5 nautical miles east of Ushuaia in the Beagle Channel, Tierra del Fuego, Argentina.

The only New Zealand lighthouse mentioned in Macías's book is the famous Stephens Island light in the Marlborough Sounds, which came into service in 1894. It has one of the most powerful lights in the country, with a range of 33 km, flashing white once every six seconds from the top of the island at an altitude of 183 metres.

The Māori name of the island is Takapourewa, in recognition of the forest of takapou trees (matipou or māpou) that once stretched down to the shoreline. In 1966 the island was designated a wildlife sanctuary, and the lighthouse was fully automated in 1989, the year DOC took over administration of the refuge. Today it is overseen by DOC in collaboration with Ngāti Koata.

The Stephens Island gecko, Hamilton's frog and the tuatara continue to thrive, but the endemic Stephens Island wren was driven to extinction by Tibbles, a pet cat that accompanied one of the lighthouse keepers to the island in the 1890s. Tibbles' offspring were also implicated. Cats have now been eradicated from the island.

The Lighthouse Keeper's Wife, by Jeanette Aplin, who lived on the island with her husband Pip for six years, is a very good read.

There's something about lighthouses. No matter where I have sailed, I always felt a sense of achievement when the first faint beam of light flashed across the sky with its signature sequence. It not only gave me a sense of comfort but it confirmed that my navigation was correct and that I was making a safe passage.

CHAPTER
17

ABOUT TIME WE GOT MARRIED

We had settled into a busy routine of life — working hard, establishing a forest in our 1-acre back yard, and finally reaching the stage where we needed to retire. We were both very tired and could no longer give our best to our passengers. The business was sold, Lance was seriously committed to retirement, and I had more time to become involved in a number of environmental issues.

I was sitting at my computer one day in 2011 when Lance came up behind me, placed his hands on my shoulders, leant forward and said, 'I think it's about time we got married.'

I sat still. Did he really just say that?

'Are you asking me to marry you?'

'Yes.'

I turned and looked up at him. Of course I wanted to marry him.

'Nothing fancy,' he said. 'Let's just have a party with friends. No presents, just a really good time with lots of music.'

'How about we get married on your birthday, October third?' I suggested.

'What about the Rugby World Cup?' Lance immediately countered. 'Everyone will want to watch the game between New Zealand and Canada on the second, and the Italians are playing Ireland later that night.' I had to concede. Many of our friends are rugby followers, so we changed the date to Friday 7 October. The All Blacks were playing Argentina the next day so the timing was perfect.

Our original plan was to fly by helicopter up to Mt Titiroa, one of the most prominent mountains overlooking Manapōuri, together with the local mayor, Frana Cardno, who agreed to be our celebrant, my sister Jill, and Lance's brother and sister-in-law. We would follow up with a party at the local hotel. But typically, all did not go according to plan …

Lance had been seeing his doctor about a lack of energy. He felt exhausted all the time and was losing weight. As he gradually got worse, the doctor diagnosed a thyroid problem and began treatment. He told me that if Lance showed any signs of further deterioration, I was to ring him straight away.

A week before the wedding, Lance's health plummeted. He was rushed to the hospital and placed in isolation; his white blood cell count was zero.

After two days he was worse, with not even enough energy to hold a conversation.

'If you don't want to get married, just tell me,' I said, trying to make light of the situation. He smiled and assured me he did want to get married.

I moved down to Invercargill, staying with our friend Edith so I could be with Lance. I hung our wedding invitation on the door to his hospital room, desperately hoping we would still make it. Then Lance's specialist suggested that it might be best if we got married in Lance's isolation room, admitting only the celebrant and a nurse as our witness. We would all have to wear hospital gowns and face masks.

'Okay, we can do that,' I said. It wasn't the dream wedding, for sure, but needs must.

I raced into town to inform the registrar of marriages that we were changing the wedding location from Mt Titiroa to Kew Hospital. Paperwork completed, I returned to the hospital. Lance said the party was to go ahead in his absence, as friends and family were coming from Christchurch, Dunedin, Wellington and Melbourne. As soon as the ceremony was over, I was to drive straight back to Manapōuri and join them. Jill was organising the party with the hotel staff.

We decided not to tell anyone ahead of time about Lance being so ill. Jill would let them know when they arrived.

—

THURSDAY LUNCHTIME, the day before the wedding, Edith and I were sitting in a café when my phone rang.

'Hello, Ruth, I'm ringing with an update on Lance.' It was his specialist. 'His white blood cells are recovering.'

'That is wonderful — does this mean he's on the mend?'

'Yes. A big improvement. How would you like to take him home tomorrow afternoon and get married in Manapōuri?'

'What? You're going to let him come home for the wedding?'

'Yes. You can pick him up around three, take him home for the wedding, then bring him back to the hospital. Will that work for you?'

Would it work for us?! 'Thank you, thank you — that is terrific! Wow — how fabulous!' My eyes were brimming with tears.

'Better get everything organised then!' he said before he hung up.

Edith and I couldn't believe it. Lance and I were now going to get married at the hotel in Manapōuri.

So much to reorganise! First, I was straight down to the

registry office to change the location — again. The woman had been grumpy the first time and she was no happier now.

'This is the last time you can change your venue as time is running out,' she said sternly as she handed me the revised paperwork.

Then I was off to Hallensteins to buy Lance a shirt and new jeans. He had lost so much weight none of his clothes would fit him. The dear man who was serving me loaded me up and told me to bring back whatever we didn't need. 'Just pay me when you come back,' he said with a smile. 'I'm really pleased to be able to help dress the groom.'

I jumped in my car, drove back to the hospital and raced into Lance's room with my arms full of clothes. We were both very excited. We picked out a shirt and a pair of jeans that fitted perfectly except they were too long. 'No worries, we'll get them taken up,' I said confidently. I knew there was a tailor just along from Hallensteins.

The tailor was closing for the day when I pulled up. I called out to him, 'Please! Please — just a small job. Please, we're getting married tomorrow!' He looked at me, smiled and opened the door. I quickly told him the story. 'We just need these taken up,' I said, pushing the jeans towards him.

'So, you're getting married tomorrow. Congratulations. This will only take me a few minutes. Come in.'

True to his word, he cut and quickly stitched the hems before handing the jeans back to me. 'No charge; glad to help you both.' I gave him a huge hug.

Only now did I start to believe we would truly be getting married in front of our friends and family the very next day.

Back in Manapōuri, I found that many of our out-of-town guests had already arrived, including Lance's son Dane from Melbourne. I took Dane aside. 'I have a job for you,' I said. 'You are to drive down to Invercargill tomorrow afternoon and pick up your dad from the hospital.' Dane looked stricken. I filled him in on what had happened over the past week, which all sounded unbelievable when I said it out loud.

'You need to get him home in time to have a bath and get dressed. He'll be very tired, and don't be too shocked at how much weight he has lost. He's on the mend now.'

My dear sister had everything organised at the hotel — flowers, food, music, wine, the table settings. Frana the celebrant was delighted that she wasn't going to be marrying us in a hospital room. My son Andrew was going to drive me to the hotel in my Fiat 500, and everyone who had a guitar was to bring it along.

As guests arrived, we told them what had happened over the week prior. Everyone was delighted to hear that Lance was getting better and would be able to attend *his own* wedding.

All that was left was for me to find something to wear! Some time ago Lance had bought me a beautiful black and gold dress with matching black trousers. I had never had an opportunity to wear it, but now was the time. My nieces

Courtney and Phoebe decided they would do my hair, and even paint my fingernails, helping me relax with a glass of wine and some nibbles.

—

DANE AND HUNTER, Lance's brother, collected the groom from the hospital, and how wonderful it felt to have him home.

'Guess what, Bunny,' he said as he hugged me. 'I'm allowed to stay home for the weekend. I seem to be getting better all the time.'

That was the best wedding present: we would be spending our first night together as Mr and Mrs Shaw.

I stood and watched him undress for his bath. As he unzipped his trousers he looked at me and said, 'I have another surprise for you — hope you like it.' He dropped his trousers and I saw a urine bag attached to his thigh. He had a catheter.

'Not the greatest thing to have on our wedding night,' he said with a smile.

I laughed. It really didn't matter.

Everything was ready: all I had to do was get dressed. The dress top fitted perfectly, but when I put on the trousers they were miles too long. There was no time to take them up. I had a pair of black shoes with a small heel but they hardly made any difference to the length. I tried rolling the trousers up but they looked terrible. I considered just cutting the hems off but Jill convinced me this was not a good idea. 'Stick them up with cellotape,' she said. 'No one will know.' So that's what we did.

On 13 October 1967 Lance and I had first got engaged on Stewart Island, and now, on 7 October 2011, we were finally getting married. I still had the wedding ring we had had made in 1967. I had been carrying it with me for 40-plus years.

It was a simple ceremony. Lance's promise to me:

> *Ruth, although we have had really testing times over the last 27 years our love has kept us together. You know, no matter what, I will always be there for you. It is my role in life to promote you in any direction you choose and to help you achieve your goals. I promise to always try and protect you from others and even yourself.*

His promises have been kept; he is my protector, my best friend, my PA, my travel mate, my lover, my everything.

My promise to Lance:

> *Lance, today you become my husband. I want to know what you ache for, what your dreams are, and what you long for. I want to share the adventure of retirement with you, to help you*

> *spend our money renovating our home and going on holidays, and keeping the racing yacht and Fiat in great condition. I want to share being alive and happy with you, and at times share sadness. You were my first love and today I am becoming your wife. I promise to care for you and love you always.*

Now, as I write this, we have been married for 13 years. I suppose we qualify as old — Lance is 81 and I am 78. For me, my love for Lance is renewed every day. It does not have the emotional rush of young love, but my heartbeat still quickens when I see him.

He is the love of my life.

TALES FROM THE BOOKSHOPS: THE BOOKSELLER KRAYZ

—

JENNY MY PUBLISHER was right! She had been all along. Lance is always telling me to 'just listen to what Jenny tells you'. Jenny Hellen has been publishing books for decades. In 2019 she was made publishing director of Allen & Unwin, which has won the prestigious Publisher of the Year award several times. She is now A&U's Publisher at Large, so yes, I should definitely listen to her. Jenny told me over and over that *The Bookseller at the End of the World* would be a top seller, whereas all I could think of was piles of unsold books under my bed, in the wardrobes, and hidden in all corners of our home.

Jenny was right, and my second book, *Bookshop Dogs*, is also a bestseller. I have to pinch myself sometimes. The upshot is that my bookshops have become a bit of a destination. I even get tour coaches pulling up!

One day, after a rush of customers wanting books signed and their photo taken with me — and sometimes 'lovely Lance' as well — a stunning woman strode into the shop. Her smile reached her dark eyes, which were mischievous. She radiated confidence, and we quickly slipped into conversation. Her name was Freydi — Fred for short — and she lived in Melbourne.

'Fred was my mother's nickname,' I said.

'I did notice that you dedicated your book to your mother Freda. That is really special.'

She went on to tell me that there was a copy of *The Bookseller* in the B&B where they were staying. Realising that they were just down the road, she wanted to come and meet me. She bought a copy of the book, and we continued to chat some more. 'See you again some time,' she said when she left.

Fred emailed a few times, and when Lance and I decided to visit our son Dane and his family in Mornington, just out of Melbourne, I let her know. Maybe we could have coffee or a meal together?

Little did I know that when Fred had returned home after her trip to New Zealand in January 2023 she had set up a WhatsApp group called *The Bookseller Krayz*. *Krayz* is the Yiddish word for circle. She encouraged all her friends to join the circle and read my book. They would take turns to read her copy, and when they had finished they were to make an online comment before passing the book on to the next reader.

And so my book travelled around the ever-growing group.

When Fred heard that Lance and I were coming to Melbourne she went into top gear and notified everyone in the group:

Freydi: Come MEET The Bookseller herself —

author RUTH SHAW! OOO

> *Ruth will be visiting family on the Peninsula next month.*
> *She has set aside time to meet 'as many of us' as can attend –*
> *6pm Sunday May 21st . . .*
> *Venue will be Royal Hotel Mornington (Ruth's son and daughter-in-law lease the hotel)*

It was all arranged. Fred emailed the day before we met:

> *While I mentioned that not all the ladies know each other . . . I didn't tell you that those coming to meet you are all Jewish . . . so there will be a lot of creative conversation. (I just wanted to warn you.)*

For some reason I was nervous as Lance and I waited at the Royal for the women to arrive. The restaurant staff had set up a special table in what used to be the function room and was in the process of being converted into an Asian restaurant.

We had invited one or two others as well, and Lani was the first to arrive. We had known her for nearly 10 years as she used to be a chef at the Royal. Then the others started to arrive: Debs, Sue, Fred, Tomi . . . all with gifts for me. The chatter started straight away, combined with hugs and laughter. They call themselves 'bad Jews', or 'The Badgers', as they only go to synagogue a couple of times a year.

Dane arrived with our youngest granddaughter, Chloe. The wine started to flow, and Dane ordered the food, ensuring that a wonderful assortment of entrées appeared on our table over the next half-hour.

The evening went by quickly and some lasting friendships were made. It never ceases to amaze me just how many people my book has touched.

Jenny the publisher was right. I really should listen to her.

CHAPTER
18

DETAINED IN DUBAI

Almost a year after our wedding I kissed Lance goodbye one July day and left for overseas on my own. We both wished he was coming with me but he wasn't feeling a hundred per cent and didn't want to risk getting sick again. I was flying to Moscow to visit Dmitri and Mila for a few days, then on to Riga in Latvia to meet up with my cousin Alison, to spend two weeks with her in the Baltics.

My diary outlines that I had budgeted 57 euros a day(!); my flights and travel insurance cost NZ$3640. I'm glad I kept diaries, as so much happened on this trip.

Airline staff at Christchurch Airport photocopied

my Russian visa. I was flying to Sydney, on to Bangkok, through Dubai and then to Moscow.

We landed in Dubai at 5.35 a.m. and I must have walked more than a kilometre to reach the departure lounge for the flight to Moscow.

I presented my ticket and passport prior to boarding for Moscow, and that's when I was told there was a problem with my visa. 'Please stand over there,' I was ordered. This scenario was all too familiar and my heart sank.

A uniformed man told me I would not be boarding the flight, and I was to follow him. No explanation. He agreed to ring Dmitri for me, to tell him what was happening.

I was taken down a number of floors by lift. All I had was my shoulder bag and my small leather travel pouch hanging under my clothes, where I kept my passport, credit cards, some cash and a few sachets of emergency coffee. But the authorities upstairs had kept my passport — should I be worried about that?

And where was my luggage? The uniformed man told me it had been unloaded and placed in a 'secure area'. Luckily, I always have a spare pair of pants and a small toilet bag in my shoulder bag, plus reading glasses, a small travelling laptop, my camera, and of course a book, a couple of pens and my diary.

The man walked past a row of empty offices and finally came to the end of a long corridor. He unlocked the double doors and showed me into a room filled with chairs. I noticed there were no windows. Without speaking he pointed to a chair, so I sat down as he went to speak to another guard. I looked around to see several men I took to be other detained passengers up near the front of the room, some sitting on the floor, others lounging in chairs. I was the only female and the only European, but even so I was not worried.

My escort left, nodding to me as he went past. Then one of the other detained passengers came up to me, introducing himself as Mohammad. His English was perfect. He told me we were all 'detainees', apparently with no right to leave until we had been interviewed. We would be held for as long as the authorities deemed necessary.

He introduced me to the others, mainly from African and Asian countries. Some were suspected of having false passports. One was a refugee from Sudan who had rowed a small dinghy for five days with his brother to escape the fighting in their country. Even though he had an Italian passport, which he had received legally through refugee authorities, and had evidence that his brother was already in Italy, he was about to be deported back to Sudan.

Two Muslims were under suspicion of being terrorists. Mohammad was waiting for someone to come from the British Embassy to help him, as he held a British passport.

'Why are you here, Ruth?' he asked.

'I have no idea,' I replied. 'I think it's something to do with my Russian visa. What happens now?'

'You wait to be interviewed. That's all you can do.'

'How long will it take?'

'I have been here ten days, the young man from Sudan nearly a week. Others come and go,' he said quietly. 'You just have to wait.'

I was given a blanket and one meal ticket redeemable at McDonald's. I don't know what we were supposed to do for the other meals. Hot and cold water were available so I asked who would like a cup of coffee, as I had my stash of coffee bags. Everyone said yes.

Mohammad said it would be best if, being the only woman among them, I got permission to sleep up on the main terminal floor, as the rest of them were locked in overnight. He felt it would be safer for me. I was given permission, on condition that I returned at 6 a.m. I was obviously being treated better than the men, who had all been strip-searched on arrival and had nothing with them but the clothes they were wearing.

When they let me out for the night, the first thing I did was ring Lance. It was just after midnight in New Zealand and I prayed that he would answer, which he did.

He was desperate to know why I was being held, but as I didn't know myself, there was nothing I could tell him. As to when they would release me — who knew? All I could do was reassure him that I was safe. I also rang Mohammad's wife in England to let her know where he was, as she hadn't heard from him for 10 days.

I bought a pile of sandwiches for everyone and was waiting at the door to the detention room at 5.55 a.m. Many of them were still asleep on the floor, wrapped in their single blanket.

The guards arrived and began interviews. Mohammad was to be sent back to England.

Finally, it was my turn.

Three uniformed men sat across the desk from me in the small interview room. One was holding my passport.

With no preamble he stated firmly, 'We are flying you back to New Zealand today. We will organise your tickets and let you know what time the flight departs.'

'Why am I being sent back to New Zealand?' I quietly asked. 'Why can't I go to Latvia to meet my cousin?'

'We don't have to give you any reason.'

I needed to control this situation. They had to tell me why I was there. Maybe I could turn things around by asking a question, I thought. I looked the man in the eye and said, 'Isn't it wonderful that Emirates supports New Zealand in the America's Cup? Do you watch it?'

He smiled at me and nodded. Then — incredibly — we were talking about yachting. I think he was surprised that I had been following the racing. But I had, and I knew that in the AC45 World Series being raced in Newport, Rhode Island, New Zealand had just been placed second overall. I could see the man relaxing as he settled back in his chair.

After a few moments he flicked through my passport and asked, 'So would you prefer to fly to Copenhagen, Glasgow or Amsterdam?' Bingo.

I chose Copenhagen, as I could then get a short flight across to Tallinn, Estonia, where there would be a Russian Embassy. I could still possibly get to Moscow.

He arranged for me to fly out the next morning.

'Your luggage will be waiting for you in Tallinn, and your tickets will be here soon.'

I thanked him and returned to the main room.

As I was waiting for my tickets to be delivered, a very stoned Dutch guy was brought in, swearing at the police who had him handcuffed. After kicking aside a couple of chairs he slumped down beside me. Aware that he could speak English, I introduced myself and told him to settle down and be quiet. 'If you want to get out of here quickly you have to be polite. Up to you.' We didn't hear another word from him.

I was permitted to go out to use the telephone again to ring Lance. He was relieved to hear I was back on track.

After my tickets and passport were returned to me I was permitted to spend another night in the departure lounge. I gave the young Sudanese man my meal voucher and my blanket. I wonder what happened to him.

I emailed Lance with an update. I had no plans for when I arrived at Tallinn but I didn't care. My luggage would be there, and as I had been in the same clothes for three days I was looking forward to a shower and a change of outfit.

The flight was excellent. It was a very small plane and I discovered I'd been placed in first class! It felt surreal after being in detention with a single blanket.

—

MY LUGGAGE HAD NOT arrived in Tallinn but I was assured by the lost luggage staff that they never lost luggage. Never. It would be at the airport the next day.

I had a few American dollars with which I managed to pay for a taxi and two nights' cheap accommodation. I also had my travel card. It seemed that everything in my price range was fully booked so the taxi driver took me down to the docks and found me a room in a very old, sleazy hotel, which I discovered quite quickly was a brothel. I wasn't in the least bit worried, except that as I wasn't renting the room on an hourly basis I had to pay top dollar for the two nights, but it was still very cheap.

I shared the single shower with a number of girls, many of whom I could tell were Russian. The facilities were extremely basic. There were no ceiling panels in the bathroom or toilet so you could see the plumbing, and the floors were bare concrete. At least my bed was cosy.

Thankfully the young man at the desk spoke a little English, and he pointed me in the direction of the market where I could buy some cheap clothes. I also needed a bank as I had no local currency. After buying a skirt, underwear, sandals, two tops and a large T-shirt to sleep in, I was back off to the airport to pick up my luggage.

'Luggage not here, come back tomorrow,' I was informed by a very uninterested man.

I sighed. 'Where is it, do you know?'

'Maybe still in Dubai. Not lost — we don't have lost luggage.'

'But it *is* lost! You don't know where it is, so it is lost!'

'NOT LOST!' And with that he slammed the door.

I headed to the Russian Embassy in Pikk Street. The massive wooden door was locked but there was a small speaker on the doorframe. I pleaded in English to be let in. A woman came to the door, took my passport and signalled to me to follow her.

She disappeared behind a glass screen, checked my passport, then picked up a telephone, pointing to the telephone next to me.

I picked up the receiver only to hear her yelling, 'NO, NO, NO!' She slipped my passport back to me through the small window and hung up. With a stiff finger she pointed to the door, turned and left the room.

It didn't look like I was going to Moscow.

The next day at the airport there was still no sign of my luggage.

'NOT LOST! Just not here yet.' This was not reassuring.

I needed to confirm my flight to Latvia, which was booked for the next day. I had arranged to meet up with my cousin and her friend at our pre-booked accommodation at the university.

The Estonian customer service man looked at my tickets and, after checking his computer, told me all my flights had been suspended. They were no longer valid.

'What? They must be! I have paid for them.'

'Sorry, madam, your tickets are not valid. Have you been in some sort of trouble with the authorities?' he asked.

I told him about my time in Dubai.

'Ah, that explains it. They aways suspend your flights. You will have to find a travel agent and buy new tickets.'

'You mean *all* my tickets, even back to New Zealand?'

'All suspended.'

There were no public telephones at the airport and no internet connection available. I eventually found a travel agency and explained my predicament. They generously gave me a phone and a computer to use. Poor Lance was woken up again in the middle of the night.

'What drama now, love?'

'Rather a major drama,' I replied, and filled him in.

'Not to worry,' said good old Lance. 'I'll get it sorted with the travel insurance company.'

And he did. Incredibly, even though it was around 1 a.m., a woman answered the phone, listened to the problem and assured Lance she would sort it out. Within the hour he rang me back to say she had. All my tickets had been reinstated and I was back on my flight to Latvia tomorrow.

As I was still at the airport I went to the (not!) lost luggage counter. Of course my luggage still had not turned up. I asked them to forward it, if and when it did turn up, to me in Latvia.

Then I lost my reading glasses! I was trying so hard to remain positive but losing my glasses meant I couldn't read, let alone write. After searching the airport I went back to the market and bought a cheap replacement pair. I considered this a big tick on the positive side of the ledger.

—

THE VERY SMALL plane to Riga was run by Scandinavian Airlines. It had the capacity to carry 48 passengers but there were only 20 of us on board. On landing, I jumped on a bus to travel to the address Alison had given me, but the bus driver couldn't understand me, and also insisted I pay in Latvian rubles, not euros. A lovely local woman stepped up and paid my fare for me.

I urgently needed a bank, another T-shirt and blouse and a jersey, as I had no idea whether my luggage would ever be found. Although I had shown the bus driver the name of the university where we were staying, he forgot all about me until the end of the route, long past my stop. He wanted to throw me off the bus at that point but another driver intervened and got me back on board, this time to be dropped off a block away from the university. My cousin and her friend were already there.

The three of us explored the city over the next two days, while I continued to ring the airport twice a day to be told that my luggage was still 'not lost', but also not found.

On the third day the woman at the desk where we were staying told me my luggage had finally arrived and was out at the airport. I leapt in a taxi, located the right counter at Riga Airport and yes! I was told my suitcase had arrived — apparently via Russia.

I was asked to follow a Customs officer down a corridor to a scanning machine. Lying on a desk was my very battered suitcase. After putting it through the scanner, the man picked it up and led me down another hallway to an empty room where he produced a massive pair of bolt cutters.

I tried to tell him I had a key to open the suitcase but he ignored me and snapped the small lock in half. He then unpacked the entire contents, shaking out clothing, opening presents I had bought for Dmitri and his family, and spreading everything across the floor. He left me for a few minutes, then returned with a large middle-aged woman dressed in a similar uniform. In very broken English she asked me to accompany her into a small adjoining room. No windows, a steel chair the only furniture.

'Off clothes!'

I stared at her, not quite believing what I had heard.

'Off clothes!' she shouted again.

'I want an English-speaking woman in here with me, please,' I said assertively.

She shook her head. I wondered if she had even understood me.

'And a nurse if you are going to carry out an internal examination, please,' I continued.

'Nyet!'

I stood still, making full eye contact, not wanting her to see that inside I was about to fall apart. Was this really happening? What the hell was going on?

'OFF CLOTHES!' she yelled for a third time.

I stood naked in the middle of the bare room, hugging myself with folded arms, and started to cry.

The woman walked around me, not touching me, then opened the door and walked out without a word, slamming the door behind her. I quickly got dressed, raced back to the adjoining room, repacked my suitcase and left. No one tried to stop me.

I met up with Alison and Robyn, feeling extremely stressed and anxious. As planned, we caught the train to Sigulda, about an hour from Riga. The long carriage was nearly empty so the three of us spread out over the seats at one end, near a door. Just as the train was pulling away from the station an elderly woman carrying a basket entered our carriage. She glanced around and then, with no hesitation at all, she walked the length of the near-empty carriage and came to sit beside me. Alarm bells started to ring. Robyn panicked, stating quite loudly in English that the woman must be a spy. Alison, who was sitting on the other side of me, just raised her eyebrows.

The woman pulled a small prayer book out of her pocket and she started to talk to me in Russian. I gathered that her name was Nada. With my small English–Russian dictionary I tried to converse politely with her, thinking all the time that surely if she had been sent to follow me, she would be an English speaker. It seemed to me the best way forward would be to give her the benefit of the doubt and be friendly.

In her high-sided basket she had a packed lunch that she wanted to share with us, but Robyn was so convinced that she was a KGB agent she refused. As Nada was sorting out the food, Alison conveyed to me through hand signals that we should get out at the next stop and not carry on to Sigulda. If Nada followed us, then we knew we had a problem.

As soon as the train stopped, we grabbed our gear and got off, waving to Nada as the train pulled away. We found accommodation in the small town and, dizzy with relief, I threw myself onto my bed. I had to put this whole crazy business behind me.

I was certain that it was because of our friendship with Dmitri that I had been detained in Dubai. My name obviously was on an airport watchlist, and all seemed to stem from that.

CHAPTER
19

FAREWELL MOSCOW

IT WAS NOT until nearly a year later when I was leafing through my passport that I discovered that the page with my Russian visa had been torn out. The woman in the Russian Embassy in Tallinn must have removed it.

When we first met Dmitri I had never heard of the word 'oligarch'. I was naïve about Russian history, but I was now interested in the political situation. I learnt that privatisation initiatives under President Boris Yeltsin in the 1990s saw Russian citizens granted vouchers, representing company shares, as the state pledged to transform state-owned enterprises into collectively owned profit-making businesses.

This was a golden opportunity for people who understood the system, but many others sold their vouchers for a pittance, and there were plenty of eager buyers. Soon some individuals were acquiring large shareholdings in oilfields and refineries, vodka distilleries, coalmines, natural gas facilities and many other state-owned companies.

The increasing privatisation that followed the dissolution of the Soviet Union in 1991 was the pathway for the establishment of the oligarchs, men who rapidly accumulated vast wealth and increasing political influence.

In 2000 when Vladimir Putin became president he offered the oligarchs a deal. Essentially he told them that as long as they respected his authority, he would turn a blind eye to their mansions, super-yachts and private jets. Over time, those who complied continued to do very well. Those who worked to undermine Putin could find themselves thrown into prison or forced into exile, or they died/disappeared under suspicious circumstances.

The more I learnt about this, the more I came to believe that this was how Dmitri had become the very successful businessman he clearly was. The fact that he despised Putin put him in danger.

Two very good books about Putin and the corruption in Russia are *Red Notice* and *Freezing Order* by Bill Browder. Browder was an American financier who worked in Russia from the 1990s. He soon learnt that theft was rampant among oligarchs profiting from the privatisation occurring in the former Soviet Union. While investigating a $230 million tax fraud perpetrated against his company by Russian government officials, Browder's lawyer, Sergei Magnitsky, was imprisoned, tortured and killed. In response, Browder successfully lobbied the US Congress to pass the Magnitsky Act, which aimed to freeze the assets of those involved in human rights violations. The Magnitsky Act has expanded beyond the United States to other nations — and has made Browder a target of the Kremlin.

—

WE WENT BACK to Russia twice more. Both times I was held up as my passport was carefully checked. Lance went straight through and had to wait while the authorities considered whether to allow me entry. It was like a game — they were trying to embarrass me, show me who was in charge, so I just smiled and told them not to hurry. In 2014, when we visited, Putin was in his third presidential term. This was the year Russia invaded the Crimean Peninsula, which was part of Ukraine, and then annexed it. Putin declared that his goal was to 'demilitarise and denazify' Ukraine.

Russia felt different. Wherever we went, we had to hand over our passports for inspection. Armed security guards, many with dogs, patrolled the streets, the trains and the entrances to many of the shopping malls. The freedoms of ordinary Russians were being taken away.

Dmitri told us quietly that under no circumstances were we to speak about politics, ask about his business ventures or mention Putin's name, unless we were in 'a safe place'. Even in his car, conversation was strained. Who could he trust? Where was safe? Our stay was short and mercifully uneventful.

Four years later we went back again. I had been speaking to Dmitri on Zoom and was very concerned as he often broke down and cried. Our conversations were brief with no substance; all we could offer was our friendship. We spoke in innuendos, always aware that he was possibly being bugged. I wanted to see him in person.

Dmitri was waiting for us at the airport. He had lost 15 kilograms but was still a big man. Since our last visit we discovered that Dmitri had lost his businesses to Putin — 'stolen' was the word he used. The government claimed he owed US$300,000 in tax, even though he had proof that he had paid tax in full over all his years in business. He was one of many former businessmen now living through this nightmare. Several of his friends had been imprisoned; others had fled Russia, leaving everything behind.

Dmitri was not permitted to work, to leave Russia or to personally own anything. He had signed his two homes, his vehicles and apartment over to his mother and wife, and was now a house husband. He had to borrow a friend's car to pick us up from the airport.

Since we were last there, hundreds of high-rise buildings had been built; 15 million people now lived within a 60-kilometre radius of central Moscow. Dmitri talked about the corrupt government siphoning billions of dollars out of the country and how the Russia he loved was reverting to the pre-1991 Soviet days. He was convinced it was only going to get worse. The gap between the rich and poor was growing, people were frightened, many no longer felt safe.

Dmitri felt imprisoned in his own country, his 'non-worth' a hard pill to swallow. Where previously he had been a happy, hardworking, proud Russian, now he was drinking heavily, and there was a sadness in their home.

He was concerned for his children. Russia, his homeland, was no longer a country in which he wanted them to be raised. And yet, although he had passports for two other countries, he didn't want to leave his elderly mother behind.

We left Moscow at the end of that visit very concerned for Dmitri and his family. We would certainly not be returning while Putin was in charge. Even to us as visitors the place did not feel safe.

—

FOUR YEARS LATER, in 2022, we sent a brief email to Dmitri. Russia had recently invaded Ukraine and we wanted him to know we were thinking of him. Dmitri's mother was Ukrainian.

He replied briefly a week later, sending his love and photos of the family.

Our next communication was from Mila, saying that Dmitri been found dead on the floor of their apartment. We replied immediately, only sending our condolences out of concern that her emails were being monitored.

Just over two months later Mila wrote again to say she was now out of Russia and living in another country with her children.

We'll never know exactly what happened to our Russian friend, who had been stripped of everything. We do not believe he would have committed suicide, as he was so devoted to his wife and family.

TALES FROM THE BOOKSHOPS: MY FANATICAL BOOK FINDERS

ANGIE WORKED FOR us in the office at Fiordland Ecology Holidays and she was wonderful. Many years after we had sold our business, I met her again by chance when I was speaking at the Dunedin Public Library. Our friendship was renewed, and I also met Carol, a retired woman who reads more books than anyone I know. She read 138 books last year! She reads as much as possible during the day as she finds it difficult to see well enough at night. I wonder when her housework gets done?

One day a white van pulled up outside the bookshops and out climbed Angie and some friends. They were popping in to say hi and to drop off a few books. One of them, Wendy, offered me a small cup of red jelly that she told me was laced with strawberry sambuca. She had tipped a whole bottle into the strawberry jelly mix. I declined the offer, even after Lance said how nice it was. I was working!

They dropped off a couple of boxes of books and went on their way. This was the start of Angie and Carol's Edmonds baking powder approach to finding books for me — the number of books was sure to rise! Over the next few years they would turn up from Dunedin with a car full of books and stay with us for a couple of nights, or sometimes my friend Steve from Time Traders would drop in to their place while he was in Dunedin and pick up some boxes.

My telephone rings. 'Hi, Ruth, Angie here!' There's a small giggle, followed by: 'Carol has seven boxes of books for you. They're all good books — some really exciting ones.' I know they will be, as their books have always been exactly what I want for my shops. They never want payment, insisting that any money I owe them is paid straight to Blind Low Vision New Zealand.

My sister Jill has been a regular supplier of books since I started eight years ago. She *loves* picking up second-hand children's books for my shop, and general New Zealand books as well. When my shelves are fully stocked and I have backup stock stuffed tightly into the bookshelves in my office I tell her, 'No more books until I ring you!'

I don't know why I bother, as she just carries on buying books, totally ignoring me.

'Once it gets busy you'll want them. They're just lovely — wait till you see them,' she says with a hint of excitement. They are always 'just lovely', and yes, she is right, I do sometimes ring her in a panic wanting more books when I run short.

Then there is Inger, Sarah and Dave, Aunty Shona (not my aunty) and Rebecca, all of whom drop off random books they want to sell; and I have to mention the children who come loaded up with books they have outgrown. They have already learnt the art of swapping, or they wait impatiently for me to work out how much money they will get so they can run into the Children's Bookshop to spend it.

The problem is that my bookshops are very small, so I have to be extremely careful with what I buy. The trouble with me is that I keep seeing books that I want to read, or that are so beautiful, and I can't resist . . . Sometimes they are not even the right type of book for my shops.

Take, for instance, the two-volume *A History of the Scottish Highlands, Highland Clans and Highland Regiments: With an Account of the Gaelic Language, Literature and Music*, published in 1883. It is so *beautifully* bound in red leather.

Or two volumes of *The Great War: The Standard History of the All-Europe Conflict* by H.W. Wilson and J.A. Hammerton, published in 1916, again bound in red leather.

Not to mention the 26-volume Time-Life set of *The Old West* by D.W. Torrance, published in 1973. I dislike cowboy movies and books, but these were so beautiful I had to have them!

I am supposed to be downsizing. This obviously isn't happening, as I now have new library shelves taking up a whole wall in my office, reaching from the floor to near the ceiling. It is already nearly full.

I think my small bookshops, and all that they entail, are well and truly out of control.

CHAPTER
20

THE ANNUAL OTAGO CAVALCADE

With my cousin David and my sister Jill, Lance and I have attended the Otago Cavalcade every year since 2014, apart from the Covid years. The first cavalcade back in 1991 involved 220 people and 240 horses. It retraced the historic journey of the Cobb & Co coach from Dunedin to the Dunstan Goldfield, via the Dunstan Trail. It still runs annually, starting off in a different small town each year and generally following old trails through farmland, through small communities and over some of the lower mountain ranges. In 2023 there were more than

400 riders on horseback, as well as horse-drawn wagons, walkers and cyclists.

We take part in the cavalcade market day at the end of the ride and always seem to have a fantastic and memorable time.

David is a seasoned 'swap meet'/antiques/second-hand events man. For as long as I can remember he has scoured garage sales in Christchurch, and has belonged to the Christchurch Antique Bottle and Collectables Club. He attends selling events all over Canterbury, his SUV stacked with banana boxes full of goodies to sell, all of which have been cleaned, repaired (if necessary) and priced. His trailer is permanently laden with trestles, a small marquee, gardening equipment, tools, ladders and sometimes tables and chairs. David's stall is a magnet for anyone wanting something different — a milk-bottle carrier with the original glass bottles, old eggbeaters, antique bottles, restored tools, Kiwi memorabilia, beautiful old New Zealand woollen blankets.

Jill is a fabric artist. Her stall is covered in items made from hand-dyed wool: small embroidered scenes of Central Otago tucked into attractive frames, felted jackets and knitted jerseys for children, knitted pocket pets, beautiful small blankets for cat beds, individually designed cushion covers, book bags and felted booties. It's the colours that attract people, and the intricate handiwork of exquisite flowers, trees, mountains and sunsets.

Then there is me, my tables full of second-hand books mainly relating to the Otago area, along with books about hunting, fishing, tractors, trains, farming, New Zealand history, natural history and more.

—

WE SET UP early in the morning, well before the gates open to the public, but somehow people always start milling around before we're ready and the three of us are flat out for the entire day. We love the buzz, the hundreds of people, and of course we look forward to the arrival of the horses, bikers and walkers who have completed the trail.

On this particular morning we were set up nice and early, sitting on our deckchairs having a coffee before the early rush. We know many of the other stallholders so there was a lot of chatter and laughter between us.

A young man pulled up in his truck and started to unload his trestles and gear right beside — and partially behind — Jill's stall. He lifted a beautiful bushy plant, just under a metre high, out of the truck.

'Mind if I put this down here while I set up my marquee?' he asked me, as Jill was busy.

I couldn't help noticing he was holding a lush marijuana plant. How interesting! 'No problem,' I replied.

He placed the 'pot' plant on Jill's stall and started to set up his gear.

'What is that on my table?' asked Jill when she looked up.

'Just a weed. Marijuana. Looks very—' I started to reply.

'*No!* Not on my table! Get it off! I'm not even going to look at it.'

'It's okay, Jill, it's probably—'

'I'm not interested!' And she walked away.

The plant sat there for about 20 minutes. David, Lance and I were laughing, while Jill stood well away from her stall with her back to us.

'The plant's gone!' Lance eventually shouted to Jill. 'He's moved it.'

As we had thought, the man confirmed that the plant was being grown for medicinal use. He had information pamphlets to give the steady stream of people who came to his stall, all very interested in the plant that stood proudly on his table.

—

WAIKAWA, INLAND FROM Balfour, hosted the 2024 cavalcade. We had arranged to stay in a B&B for two nights, arriving on the Friday afternoon. We were greeted by Joan, the owner, a sprightly 83-year-old, who made us welcome. Walking into her place was like stepping back in time. The magnificent homestead had four large bedrooms, a dining room, a massive lounge and a kitchen that immediately conveyed the warmth of family life.

An electric stove sat beside the coal range but Joan told us she used the range to heat her water. I remember my grandmother doing the same when we were children. Washing would be draped around the cream and green enamel range to dry, the smell of burning coal seeped throughout the kitchen and dining room, and Gran was happy because she had lovely hot water.

We unpacked the cars and threw together a quick meal. Then Joan announced that she was going to watch the Highlanders play the Blues ('I love watching the rugby . . .'). She chatted on, naming the players, filling us in on who was playing where and what form they were in.

On Saturday morning we were away by 7.20 to set up our stalls before the fun started. The arena was already buzzing. The weather was lovely, and the Topp Twins were scheduled to play during the day and at the hoedown that evening. It was shaping up to be a great day.

And it was — we'd never been busier. We were all exhausted by late afternoon, but when we got back to our accommodation we found Joan, our host, dressed up and ready to hit the hoedown. She had the enthusiasm of a teenager.

Next morning we were having breakfast when Joan appeared, dressed in a lovely long summer dress, ready to get the day under way before she headed off to Balfour to attend Mass.

'How was your night, Joan?' Lance asked her.

'I had a great time. I bought a gin and tonic with a dash of lemon, and it was only $6!' Then we found out why it was so cheap — the alcohol content was only 4 per cent.

We listened as she told us about her wonderful evening, with everyone up dancing, and such a crowd that she never did find the friends she was supposed to meet up with.

'Then I came home and the place was in darkness!' she said.

'We were all in bed by nine,' I said.

I felt old. While we were tucked up in bed, our octogenarian hostess had been downing low-alcohol gin and tonics and dancing the night away.

TALES FROM THE BOOKSHOPS: A CONSPIRACY THEORY

—

COVID-19 BROUGHT ABOUT many challenges, which the majority of New Zealanders handled extremely well. With Prime Minister Jacinda Ardern and Director-General of Health Dr Ashley Bloomfield at the helm, the country responded quickly with border closures, lockdowns and a vaccination rollout as soon as one was available.

When I reopened the bookshops after lockdown I had to follow strict guidelines to ensure my customers remained safe and healthy. This meant a lot of additional work — cleaning every book that had been touched by a customer, washing cash, restricting the number of customers on site, and ensuring everyone had signed in and was wearing a mask.

Overall, I had no trouble with any of my customers, except one.

A middle-aged man walked towards the shops. As he wasn't wearing a mask, I stood in the doorway to block his entry.

'Please would you sign in and put on a mask.'

'I don't have to,' he replied.

'Then I'm sorry but I cannot let you into the shop.'

'It is my right to come in.'

'I am *not* letting you in, so please leave,' I stated strongly.

He stared at me and pointed his finger. 'You know why the Transmission Gully motorway in Wellington is so far behind schedule?'

This was out of left field. I didn't answer.

'I'll tell you why!' His eyes were huge and his stance was threatening — legs wide apart, chest puffed out. 'Every night the government is burying the bodies of people who have been vaccinated and died under the highway, because they don't want us to know just how many people are dying.'

He stared at me with wild eyes, waiting for a reply. When I remained silent he continued. 'You would have heard that they are having trouble with the seal on the road — it is cracking! You know why? Because the bodies are bloating!'

By now he was very agitated, particularly as I failed to respond. He jabbed his finger at me and shouted, '*THE NEXT TIME I COME HERE YOU WILL BE DEAD AND BURIED UNDER A HIGHWAY SOMEWHERE!*'

He turned and marched off, stamping his feet firmly along the footpath.

Meanwhile, I had a customer sitting inside reading a book, who had remained completely silent throughout the tirade. I sat down with a sigh of relief and looked at him. 'Wow, that was full on.'

With a smile on his face he said, 'I would never have believed you if you told me that had happened.'

'I can't quite believe it either!' I replied.

CHAPTER
21

CRITTERS IN OUR BACK YARD

Wherever I have lived, animals and birds have shared my life. Just a few days after I was born my father brought home a baby possum 'just for Ruthie'. Of course I don't remember it but apparently it lived with us at Gran's place for a few months. Throughout my childhood there were numerous cats, a large population of multi-coloured pet mice and a parrot.

When I left home, successive dogs entered my life, among them Rewa, Buka and Dylan Thomas. When I was living in Australia there were orphaned kangaroos and wallabies, and a koala with badly burnt paws, ears and nose. Timothy Roo, a grey kangaroo, represented my family at my third wedding as no one else could attend. I had reared him since he was tiny, as he was orphaned during a bush fire. He finally left home when he was much taller than me, only to return a year later with a large group of friends to drink from our water-hole when the region was experiencing a drought.

Ludmila Hoffman, a small tabby cat, and Jericho, a beautiful mongrel, were my companions when I sailed the eastern coast of Australia. Both adapted well to life at sea.

Lance also loves animals, and since we have lived together in Manapōuri our home has never been without at least one critter of some type, living either in our big back yard or inside the house.

Our seal pup

Lance answered the phone. It was someone from the Department of Conservation. A member of the public in Milford Sound had rung to report an injured seal pup in one of the public toilets.

Lance was DOC's coastal Fiordland guy, so it was up to him to drive to Milford Sound, nearly two hours away, and evaluate the situation.

He entered the toilet building quietly, closing the door behind him so as not to stress the seal pup any more than it already was. Tucked behind the toilet was a tiny, beautiful, wide-eyed seal pup that had been shot between the eyes. Lance could see the bullet wound — a clean round hole that somehow, incredibly, had not been fatal.

He gently picked up the pup and placed it in a sack. Like so many animals once they are in the dark, the pup quickly settled down.

Lance drove straight to our local vet, who X-rayed the pup and determined that the bullet had miraculously not fractured or entered its skull. The bullet must have fallen out, as it didn't show up on the X-ray. If the offender had been using a high-calibre rifle it would have been a different story.

The pup was given antibiotics and painkillers, and now needed time to convalesce. But where? Of course — there was no question as to who was going to nurse it back to health. Lance brought the seal pup home. This was a first, and I was more than a little apprehensive.

Luckily, we have a small hut down in our back yard which, after we cleaned it out, proved the perfect place for the pup to rest and recover. A local fisherman supplied us with fresh fish to feed it. Initially we put the fish through a mincer, together with the seal's medication, and hand-fed it. The house smelt of fish the entire time the pup was with us — it was ghastly — but we didn't care. Our little friend was recovering quickly. Whenever we had visitors we had to explain that we didn't have rotten fish in the fridge.

We filled a baby bath with water, hoping the seal would

enjoy having a swim, but maybe because it was fresh water the pup showed no interest.

Over the next two weeks the injury continued to heal well. The pup was eating whole pieces of fish by then, and becoming quite feisty. It was time for it to go back to Milford Sound, where we hoped it would rejoin its colony. I was sad to see it leave, as it had quickly learnt to trust us and I loved watching it explore the back yard.

Lance placed the pup in a box and drove it back to Milford. He asked his brother Hunter, one of the boat skippers in Milford, to keep an eye out for it — easily identifiable by the pale 2-cm bald circle between and just above the eyes.

Lance released the seal in the harbour, not far from where he had found it, and it was obviously extremely happy to be back in the sea. He stood and watched it diving, then surfacing to roll over and start washing itself with its fins. He left feeling confident that the pup would be fine.

During the next week Hunter caught sight of it several times lying in the sun on the rocks with the other seals. Over a period of a couple of months the scar slowly covered with fur and our seal was no longer identifiable, but we knew it had been accepted back into the fold.

Nobody was ever charged with the cowardly crime.

Some months later DOC heard from a tourism operator in Milford Sound that another seal had been shot. It was lying dead on a rock, blood running down to the sea.

Passengers on the tourist vessels were visibly distressed and many of them were taking photos.

Lance was once again called in to assess the situation, and also to try to find the culprit. He knew there was little chance of that, but nevertheless he visited every boat in the sound gathering information. One boat he boarded was owned by a local fisherman Lance knew and trusted.

'I know why you're here, Lance,' the fisherman said. 'We know who's doing this. Leave it with me.'

The offending boat, a new arrival, was advised to leave the area.

The seal pup was one of the most wonderful animals we ever had in our back yard. I will never forget its beautiful black eyes, its stiff whiskers, and the complete trust it had in us to help.

Kahu, the harrier hawk

We were driving to Te Anau when we came across an injured harrier hawk on the side of the road. Although it was still alert, it could not fly because one of its wings was drooping.

After covering it with my coat so it couldn't peck me, I gently felt along the length of the wing and decided it wasn't broken. We had a netted-off area in our back yard with a shelter at one end that we decided would be a perfect place for the injured bird to convalesce, so we carefully gathered it up and took it home.

We strapped the hawk's wing to its body and within a short time it was tucking in to the various bits of road-kill we picked up and brought home. I always approached the bird quietly, talking softly so I didn't give it a fright. I wore thick leather gloves, as it quickly learnt to jump up onto my arm. I would carry it around the back yard, chatting all the time, looking directly into its beautiful, piercing yellow eyes.

We didn't actually know what sex the bird was, but somehow I always considered it to be female, with its distinctively striped tail. We named her Kahu.

Three sides of our large back yard are enclosed by well-established trees, as the back of our home forms part of our western boundary. We knew there was a chance Kahu would never be able to fly again, but she was soon striding confidently around the back yard, obviously right at home, and returning to her covered shelter at night.

Over the next few weeks we checked the wing frequently but kept it strapped. Kahu patiently let us do this, watching every movement we made but never struggling. When we finally removed the strapping, the wing was clearly weak, but Kahu could hold it firmly tucked into her body.

There's a small hill at the end of our yard and Kahu decided this was the ideal place to practise her flying skills. We watched as she walked up the hill, turned and started running back down, raising her wings slowly. She did this numerous times over several days until finally she lifted off the ground. We were both so excited we clapped and cheered. She was flying!

There were a few weeks of flying around our back yard before we were confident enough to carry her out onto the open area in front of our home. Kahu opened her wings and flew confidently, then crashed straight into a STOP sign on the corner of our street. Thankfully she wasn't hurt, and seemed happy when we returned her to the safety of the back yard.

Weeks later, when we felt Kahu was strong, alert and flying well, we tried again. This time we took her out to the small airport on the outskirts of Manapōuri. We drove down to the end of the runway, and I then carried her on my arm to the boundary of the Kepler Mire. We had seen hawks and occasionally falcons in this area so we thought it an excellent place to release her. The airport was hardly used, as the main airport then was based in Te Anau. It was so quiet that we used the runway as a place to teach kids to drive.

Kahu stood on my glove and looked around with her wise eyes. She raised herself up on her legs, lifted her wings, and then with a strong downward push she silently lifted off. We watched as she circled above the mire, easily catching a thermal and soaring with open wings.

She had been with us for nearly two months. I cried as I looked up and waved her goodbye.

Excelsius, the southern black-backed gull

An injured black-backed gull lay on our doorstep wrapped in a towel — all I could see was part of its beak. Lance and I have become known in the district as the people to bring injured birds to, even though there is a DOC-run bird park in Te Anau where they nurse injured birds back to health.

'I think it has a broken wing,' a woman whispered. I gathered the bird into my arms, briefly thinking, 'Oh no, not another two months of wing rehabilitation . . .' After examining the wing, which was not badly damaged, we decided we would keep the gull where we had housed Kahu. It was an adult, easily identified by the red dot on the end of the beak.

I named the gull Excelsius, meaning 'high' — Celse for short. My hope was that we would soon see it fly away, just like Kahu.

But Celse was born to be a pet. It soon learnt that there was plenty of food here, so this accommodation would do nicely. After just a few days it was walking up the steps to the back door with a 'feed me' look in its eyes, at times calling in a loud screech, '*Agh, agh, agh!*'

Initially Celse made no attempt to fly, but then one day we noticed the gull standing on the lawn flapping its wings. Over the next few weeks it started to fly, a little further each day.

I was walking home from our local shop when suddenly Celse was flying right beside me, just above my shoulder, head turned to look straight at me.

'Wow! Have you come to say goodbye?'

The gull followed me to the corner, where I stopped. Celse flapped its beautiful wings and, with total confidence, flew out towards the lake.

A couple of days later I received a call from the Real Journeys office in Manapōuri.

'Ruth, we have an albatross being fed out on the grass by our passengers. It's eating bread. Is this okay?'

I knew immediately that it was no albatross, it was Excelsius. As most people consider black-backed gulls to be rowdy pests, I was reluctant to tell them that.

'Just tell them to stop feeding it and it will eventually fly away.'

That was the last we heard of Celse, our southern black-backed gull.

Ansett, the homing pigeon

'Hi, Ruth, we have a pigeon in the shop behind the counter. Can you come and get it?'

'Is it injured?' I asked.

'It doesn't look injured, but it doesn't want to leave.'

I walked down to the shop with a box, thinking I was going to be picking up a native pigeon or kererū, but there behind the counter was a grey, blue and white homing pigeon, complete with leg tags.

I placed it in the box and walked home. It was hungry

and thirsty but I couldn't see any obvious injuries. I took it down to the back yard where it settled down quietly, showing no interest in leaving. I had to try to find its owner.

All racing pigeons have coded plastic and metal rings that identify their owners. I contacted the closest racing pigeon club and read out the numbers from the pigeon's tags. Within a couple of hours someone called me back with the owner's details. The pigeon was from Christchurch but had clearly flown — or been blown — off course. By now I had named the pigeon Ansett, after the Australian airline.

The owner was thrilled that his bird had been found and asked if we could take it down to Invercargill, put it on a plane and have it flown back to Christchurch. 'Just put it in a secure box with a little food. I'll pick it up from the airport.'

Off we went on a two-hour drive to Invercargill with Ansett in a box.

'Well, job done,' I said to Lance after the plane took off. 'That was one of our easier rehabilitations!'

About a week later I pulled open the bedroom curtain and looked down our back yard.

'*Ansett!* Lance, Ansett is back!'

'Really?' Lance came to look, and sure enough, there was the little pigeon strutting around. I raced out to welcome it. 'What are you doing back here?'

Christchurch is over 500 km away, which we thought was a very long way for a small bird, but the owner, when we contacted him again, told us a fit, healthy bird can cover that distance in a day.

The owner was, once again, delighted, as Ansett was one of his best pigeons. He just couldn't understand why it kept turning up at our place. He sent a proper carrying cage for Ansett's return flight to Christchurch, and we made another trip to Invercargill for another goodbye.

'This time, Ansett, please don't come back!' said Lance as we handed the bird over.

The owner rang to thank us (again). 'I hope this is the last time,' he said.

So did we. And thankfully it was.

Twizel, Dansey, Woodstock and Celmisia, the guinea pigs

Our American friend Chris was staying with us on his way back home from McMurdo Station in Antarctica, where he worked every season as an electrician. Our place was a 'stopover' haven for his first few days off the ice.

He had brought us four guinea pigs as a gift. Not that we particularly wanted guinea pigs, but as our back yard was fully fenced and almost predator free, it was a perfect home for them. Cats and stoats could not get in, and we trapped possums and rats which occasionally arrived.

We named them Twizel, Dansey, Woodstock and Celmisia and made them a little house: an upside-down drawer covered with lino to keep it dry, with a wee entrance cut into the side. We made a long, moveable wire-netting tunnel to give them access to fresh grass and somewhere safe to roam.

It appeared all four were fat, lazy, noisy males who spent fully half their time eating. Still, we grew fond of them and hated the idea of keeping them enclosed, even though we continually moved their tunnel and house around the yard.

So we set them free to roam. Initially they were timid, venturing only short distances and jumping in fright at anything unusual. But slowly they gained confidence and started exploring, nibbling the plants around the pond and under the trees. As their fitness increased, their weight dropped and they became quite agile. They could jump anywhere. Nothing was safe from their ever-nibbling teeth.

Ginger-coloured Twizel was the boss, always fighting and frequently knocking his teeth out. They regrew quite quickly — up to 2 mm a week! Dansey was long-haired and pure white. We often washed him in the sink as he was always getting muddy. He would just sit in the warm water, loving the attention. Celmisia was quiet and stayed close to his best friend Dansey, who would challenge Twizel when he got too rough.

Woodstock was the most unusual of the four, with soft grey fur over his head and shoulders and long white fur over the rest of his body. He was shy and antisocial and seemed as if he was constantly stoned (hence his name). I became increasingly worried about him being bullied so eventually I put him in with the chickens. Woodstock settled in easily and had a nest box of his own, which occasionally had a freshly laid egg in it. He would snuggle down, covering the egg with his long fur, and fall asleep.

Everyone who came to visit was entertained by the guinea pigs, who roamed around eating ferns, flaxes, saplings and grass, but still three times a day squealed out for vegetable scraps. They need high-fibre food to keep their teeth short so we fed them carrots, apples, stalks of broccoli, hay and bananas. They seemed to eat anything, including flax!

Their six-monthly checkup at the vet was always interesting. They were weighed, teeth and nails were checked, and also ears and feet. There was never anything wrong with them except for Twizel, who always had teeth missing. Twizel hated going to the vet. They lived with us for over three years, fat, happy and entertaining.

Dansey died quietly one day under his favourite flax bush. Woodstock died down by the chicken coop, Celmisia disappeared, and poor Twizel was killed by a dog that got in. Lance was so upset he cried.

The guinea pigs are buried in our back yard, together with many other birds and animals.

The bathroom aviary

Our home is very small, which is great as I hate housework. The original bathroom was just a toilet and shower with a handbasin, so small that when Lance bent over to shave, his backside stuck out the door.

The only thing I wanted to spend money on when we sold our business was a really lovely bathroom with *two* baths — a long one for Lance and a short one for me so I don't sink when I am reading. And so it came to pass, thanks to my son Andrew. We have big windows that slide open so we can watch the birds in the private back yard. On one occasion we lay in our baths and watched snow falling.

The new bathroom also proved to be a perfect place to raise baby birds. Three baby thrushes were the first occupants. I laid large plastic bags on the bottom of my bath, tipped in good dirt to a depth of about 7 cm, and piled up small branches so the birds could stand to see out over the back yard. At night I put them in a bird cage, which I covered, and on cold nights we left a heater on.

It worked really well. When they were old enough to feed themselves I would bury live worms in the dirt. The thrushes quickly learnt how to listen and catch them. Sadly, two of them died but Katherine Mansfield survived. We took to leaving the windows open so she came and went whenever she wanted. She often hung out with me when I was gardening or hanging out the washing.

Katherine Mansfield finally flew away but came back two full years later to be fed, as she was nesting in our forest. She was around for years, entertaining customers at the bookshops.

The next bird was a tomtit named Tup, who came to us very tiny and with hardly any feathers. I kept her warm by making a nest in a Turkish fez filled with warm woollen socks. Tup slept inside by the fire at night but spent the days in the bathroom, learning to fly from one branch to another. Tup became so attached to me that I had to start wearing a hat, as the little bird loved sitting on my head, which became her favourite landing place. As soon as I pulled on my woolly hat, Tup would swoop in to land on it and was happy to stay with me wherever I went.

I was certain Tup would survive but one morning when I went in the tiny bird had died. A bird's metabolism is very high, so death is often quick because of organ failure, which can be caused by a virus or accidentally consuming a toxin. I had fed Tup mealworms, which are a safe food for young bug-eating birds, but maybe not for tomtits.

Mrs B was a blackbird who, over a period of three years, would fly into the kitchen and lounge to select her own food from the fruit bowl. It began when she was nesting in a tree across the road and would arrive on our doorstep as soon as she knew we were up in the morning, waiting to be fed. We would leave the door open for her, so if we were too slow she would hop up onto the sofa and demand to be fed. If this failed, she headed for the fruit-bowl buffet on the bench and helped herself.

Her boyfriend Hoppy, who had a damaged leg, was much more polite and would just stay outside waiting for us to feed him.

When Mrs B died, one of her daughters used the same

nest across the road. She also took over from her mother in coming to us to be fed, and raiding the fruit bowl . . .

Three tiny dunnocks were found by overseas visitors down among the stones on the shoreline of the lake. It was an extremely hot day and my son Andrew was down there having a swim when he came across the girls, who showed him the fledglings.

By the time Andrew had carried them home they were very dehydrated, and felt warm in my hand. When birds are dehydrated they are unable to digest food, even if they try to eat. I keep sucrose in my cupboard for just such emergencies, so I quickly mixed some up with water and drip-fed the moisture into their eager, open beaks. Two of the dunnocks recovered quickly but the third, the smallest, took longer.

The bathroom was once again converted into an aviary, with an oil heater at night for extra warmth, even though they were tucked up in the fez. After two days they were eating insectivore mix, a rich protein powder mixed with water that is a complete food for young birds. Still unable to fly, the birds hopped around in the dirt-covered bath, frequently falling asleep under fresh small branches with green leaves.

How surprised I was when one morning I found the three of them sitting up by the window. They were flying! I refilled their food bowl, then sprinkled compost over the dirt in the bath, with worms and bugs for them to find.

The two strongest birds were flying really well and continually chatting, but the third one, which I named Duff, was well behind in development. Whenever I went into the bathroom Duff would fly onto my arm, my head or shoulder, and chat to me until I fed it by hand.

Sadly, Duff didn't make it. There were tears, as I had grown fond of the little bird.

When the other two were flying strongly I opened the bathroom windows. Within minutes they flew out into the back yard, landing on a mature beech tree. We left the windows open and placed their food dish on the windowsill just in case they needed it. Only one came back, had a huge meal and flew off again. That was the last time we recognised them as they disappeared into the trees.

I like to think the dunnocks in our garden are the fledglings we raised, and their offspring.

Diesel, the kitten

Breaksea Girl was down in Bluff where Lance was carrying out annual maintenance. As he walked back from the engineer's one day after picking up a part for the boat, he thought he heard a kitten meow. He looked under a pile of rubbish and, sure enough, there was a bedraggled black kitten. It was tiny.

Lance went back to work for the rest of the afternoon on the boat, then packed up to drive back to Manapōuri. When he looked and saw the kitten was still there, he gathered it up, wrapped it carefully in a bundle of rags and brought it with him. He knew he was creating a drama, as we both love cats but choose not to own one because we encourage birds into our garden.

Lance brought this little conundrum home to me. The all-black kitten had blue eyes, and little pepper-pot circles where his tiny whiskers sprouted. The poor thing was covered in diesel so I bathed him gently, and made up a dish of soft food with warm milk. We named him Diesel. As tiny and thin as he was, he started to purr and fell asleep.

We had no cat litter box so before bed I took him out into the garden, where he immediately dug a shallow hole and squatted. Then he covered the hole with his tiny paws. We couldn't believe it.

I was reluctant to leave him alone so I took him to bed with me to keep him warm, and so he could hear my heartbeat. Whenever we had orphan kittens or cats as children our mother would put a ticking clock in their bed as she believed it helped them settle.

Lance and I both thought Diesel was on his way to recovery, and discussed what we would do with him long term. Much as we wanted to keep him, we knew we couldn't.

One night not long afterward Diesel was warm and clean with a full tummy, and he was purring and purring. I had my hand resting on him and was talking to him when the purring stopped and he grew completely still.

He had died.

I sat up in bed and held him in disbelief. In the short time we had had him, we were both won over by this wee kitten. We tried to console each other. We had done everything we could, and at least Diesel had died happy.

The next day we made a wooden cross and wrote 'Diesel' on the crossbar, dug a hole near the base of a beech tree and placed the weightless kitten on a bed of fern fronds.

Although this happened over 30 years ago, we still talk about Diesel with sadness and love.

His grave is just across from the spot where we buried Hunza. If you have read either of my earlier books you will know about Hunza, the German shepherd who was my trusty assistant when I was a youth worker in Invercargill. Much of my success with young people was down to Hunza. He loved everyone and everyone loved him. Nothing fazed him, no one scared him.

There is a huge fern growing over his grave, and every time I go down there, tears cloud my eyes. Whenever I see a German shepherd, Hunza slips into my mind. He was a special dog.

Buffy, the bumblebee

'Nothing surprises me anymore,' Lance mumbled when I agreed to adopt an injured bumblebee he had found just outside our front door. It was missing three legs and its left wing was badly damaged, so of course he brought it inside to me.

Coincidentally, I had just finished reading *A Sting in the Tale: My Adventures with Bumblebees* by Dave Goulson, all about how bumblebees were transported to New Zealand from England by ship; their importance for pollination (more than honey bees); and why they are disappearing. I was now a lower-level authority on bumblebees, and recognised this one as a buff-tailed bee. She was not a worker bee or a male as she didn't have a white bottom.

A shoebox made an ideal bumblebee home. I covered the bottom with dead leaves and mulch and a selection of flowers for her to browse on. I was somewhat surprised when she was still alive after four days, at the point when I found another injured bee — a worker buff-tail, also with a damaged wing.

'Guess what, Lance? I've found a friend for Buffy!'

Named Barbara Buff-tail, the new addition settled in quickly. She was a lot more active than Buffy, constantly grazing on the flowers, which I now had to refresh often. I placed a small wad of paper towel soaked in honey and warm water near the flowerheads, which the bees loved — in fact they looked for it every morning. They became good companions; sometimes we could hear them buzzing to each other.

Bumblebees only live for four to six weeks, and Barbara died the morning of the general election, which was not a good start to the day. Buffy was obviously looking for her, searching among the flowers and leaves.

Meanwhile, I managed to injure my left thumb and had to wear a bulky hand support. It meant I accidentally touched Buffy one day and in surprise she stung me. It was just a tiny prick but my forefinger started to swell. The next morning as I was placing fresh flowerheads in her shoebox it happened again — she stung me again on the same finger.

My entire hand started to swell and became extremely hot. By lunchtime the swelling was creeping up my arm so Lance drove me to the medical centre. Here I was with a hand support on my left hand and now my right hand was enormous from Buffy's stings. But antihistamines are miraculous and my hand was back in action after 24 hours.

Buffy had been with us for five weeks when we packed our luggage into the car to head off on a book promotion trip to Christchurch. From there I would fly to Hawke's Bay to speak at the Readers and Writers Festival. Sitting beside me in her box in the car was Buffy, surrounded by fresh flowers, a small empty medicine bottle that had become her nesting place, and her pad of sweet honey water. It was interesting to learn so much about bumblebees. One day she would delight in seeking nectar from broom, lavender, clover flowers and dandelions; the next day she would completely ignore them, looking for something new. She needed attention every day!

I flew off to Hawke's Bay and left Lance to look after Buffy in Christchurch, awaiting my return. Needing to find fresh flowers for her daily, he spotted a wonderful garden full of blooms just down from where he was staying. He knocked on the door and asked the woman if he could cut some of her lavender and daisy heads for his pet bumblebee.

She smiled and said yes, but Lance told me she looked a little taken aback. When I got back to Christchurch we decided to take Buffy around to show the woman and thank her for the flowers. She was delighted, admitting she had found it extremely strange when a man came to her door to ask for flowers for his pet bumblebee . . .

During the seventh week I noticed Buffy was falling onto her back frequently, and was sluggish. She had lost interest in feeding. She died quietly in her shoebox, surrounded by flowers.

Michael Shoelace and Tommy Trousers, the lambs

If you have never seen an Arapawa lamb you don't really know what the word cute means. Arapawa are a rare sheep breed found mainly on Arapaoa (previously Arapawa) Island in the Marlborough Sounds. Michael Shoelace and Tommy Trousers were both stunningly handsome Arapawa.

Lance answered the phone. 'No. No, not a good idea,' he said. 'I'll hand you over to Ruth and she will say yes.'

My friend Vicky was ringing to tell me she had given my name to a local farmer, John, who was looking for someone to raise an orphan lamb. 'I thought you would love a lamb—'

'I would!' I said happily, as Lance shook his head and rolled his eyes.

'John will be ringing you today,' said Vicky. 'I knew you would say yes.'

I hung up. 'Really, Ruth!' said Lance, exasperated. 'Don't you have enough to do? You know how much work a lamb is!'

When John rang I confirmed that I would love the lamb, which would be safe in our fully fenced back yard. Within the hour he arrived with a pet carrier, inside which stood a beautiful black lamb. He had a white diamond on his forehead and a white tip on the end of his tail.

'Oh, how beautiful. What's his name?'

'Mike.'

Arapawa have long legs and a narrow face and are super active. Mike settled in really well. He played with the chickens, totally ignored Cove, the dog who lived with us part time, and soon learnt that he was welcome to come inside the house while I prepared his bottle of milk.

When Mike started to chew the shoelaces on my boots, his wee tail wagging furiously, the name Michael Shoelace came to mind, and it stuck.

Michael Shoelace was a popular guest at the bookshops. Customers would feed him his bottle and hug him; children played with him. But his favourite occupation was checking out everyone's shoes for shoelaces to chew. Three excited little girls lined up in a row one day and giggled as

Michael Shoelace methodically went from one shoe to the next, giving all the laces a good chomp.

Not surprisingly, he loved going to the bookshops.

When he was ready to be weaned, Michael Shoelace was claimed by a farming family, and went to live a happy life with his own small flock of females (but probably no shoelaces).

The following year John rang me again.

'Hi, Ruth. I have twin lambs that need a home. Interested?'

Silly question. Two male lambs turned up, only a day old, very tiny and thin. My sister had made some beautiful lamb coats out of handmade felt and embroidered with colourful flowers, and luckily I had two. I fed the babies, pulled on their new coats and tucked them into a banana box with a hot-water bottle.

The next day I took them to the vet, as both had breathing difficulties. Sadly, the bigger lamb developed pneumonia and died at only three days old. The smaller one recovered and within days was out of the banana box and following me around. He was inquisitive, energetic, noisy, demanding and extremely cuddly. Our friend Thomas from Bavaria, who was staying with us, sat with me one morning as I was bottle-feeding the unnamed lamb. As soon as the bottle was empty the lamb started to chew the bottom of Thomas's trousers, and from that moment his name was Tommy Trousers.

He was very much like a goat, jumping and leaping, playing with everyone at the bookshops. In fact one customer told me with great authority: 'Ruth, he *is* a goat. I know goats and Tommy is definitely a goat.' Yes, he did look like a goat, with his long legs and small pointed face, but he was definitely an Arapawa sheep.

When we finally weaned him he was rehomed with my doctor's family, who have a small farm.

—

THESE ARE ONLY a few of the stories about our back-yard critters. There have been more birds; Briggs and Stratton, the twin goats; Russel, our godson's pet rat; several spiders and even a black mouse. All left an imprint on us and gave us immense joy. In many cases I swear they displayed love for us. Despite the sadness and tears when they went, for me this was always a small price to pay.

TALES FROM THE BOOKSHOPS: WHAT IS IT ABOUT SUBMARINES?

I DON'T KNOW exactly when my interest in submarines started, but over the years I have collected many books on them. As a Wren in the Royal New Zealand Navy in 1963 I had the opportunity to go on board the USS *Archerfish*. I was 18. I was so excited that I went to the library to find out all about her. She was commissioned in 1943 and joined the Pacific Fleet. In November 1944 she torpedoed and sank the *Shinano*, a Japanese aircraft carrier, near Tokyo Bay. *Shinano* was the largest warship ever to be sunk by a submarine. Total lives lost were 1435.

In 1963 the *Archerfish* was in Auckland, tied alongside at the Devonport Naval Base, preparing to carry out sea trials in the Hauraki Gulf. Two Wrens had been invited to go along and I was one. As the *Archerfish* left the wharf we were standing on the foredeck, waiting for instructions from the officer on watch. When we heard the call '*Diving stations, diving stations*', we raced below.

We were in our navy-blue dress uniform, with white shirt and navy tie, stockings and heavy shoes, while the American sailors wore sensible working gear.

We were diving! I was watching everything, trying to make sense of all the dials. Here I was in the control room of a submarine, watching the crew at work! When we levelled off we were told we could go to the mess for lunch but I didn't want lunch. I wanted to stay in the control room.

'Wren, your lunch is ready in the mess. Follow the crew.'

'Sir, I would like to stay here. I can eat lunch any time but I will never have the opportunity to be on a submerged submarine again.' I looked directly at him.

He shrugged.

'Please, sir . . .'

'They have ice-cream for dessert,' he said.

'I'd still prefer to be here — sir.'

'Notify galley, one Wren not joining them for lunch,' he called to one of the crew. He then looked across at me. No smile, but he did wink.

We received a small certificate stating that we were now honorary submariners of the United States Navy, having served on the USS *Archerfish* for a day. This is the day I always remember whenever I think of my brief naval career.

YEARS LATER, WHEN Lance and I set up Fiordland Ecology Holidays, we converted the small flat adjoining our house to a B&B. The modest income kept us afloat over the first few years as we built up our business and reputation.

A middle-aged German couple booked in for two nights. They were very polite — I warmed to them quickly.

When I went to make sure they had everything they wanted, the husband asked why I had so many books on submarines. He was holding my copy of *Unbroken: The Story of a Submarine* by Alastair Mars, published in 1953. Mars first went to sea in 1932 and was a submariner during the war. In 1942 he took command of the new British submarine *Unbroken*, which sank 30,000 tonnes of enemy shipping in the Mediterranean in one year.

I told our German guest about the USS *Archerfish* and my fascination with submarines. 'It's strange because I'm a pacifist, I hate the idea of war, but I admire the courage and skills of the men on both sides.'

He looked at me and said, in his strongly German-accented English: 'I was a U-boat captain during the war.'

We looked at each other in silence. What do you say in a situation like this? Do you ask questions? There were many I wanted to ask, but I remained silent.

In the end he continued. 'I had a young, inexperienced crew and was ordered to continue operating in the North Atlantic. I knew by this time we could not win the war — U-boats were being sunk in very high numbers. I decided to hide in one of the Norwegian fiords to save my crew.'

I listened in disbelief, recognising the courage of this man standing in front me, who had stood up against Hitler. His decision had saved the lives of 45 young men, who returned safely home to Germany. We talked for over an hour. It was a conversation I will never forget.

Lance and I always look out for submarine movies. *Greyhound* is a favourite, in which Tom Hanks plays the US navy commander of a group of destroyers escorting an Allied convoy in the Atlantic to defend them against U-boats. The movie was made in 2020, based on the 1955 novel *The Good Shepherd* by C.S. Forester.

CHAPTER
22

ADDICTION

My son Andrew was on the phone.

After a few minutes of catching up I sensed that something was wrong.

'What's going on, Andrew?' I asked.

There was an extended silence.

'Jacob wants to go down and stay with you and Lance. He's home from Melbourne and wants to get off P.'

The last time we had seen our 27-year-old grandson was in Melbourne several months previously. We'd suspected at the time that he was on drugs, but P or methamphetamine has to be one of the worst.

'I'll have to talk it over with Lance,' I said. This would be a long-term commitment and we needed to know we could actually help. 'Give us a few days and then get Jacob to ring us,' I said to his father.

We knew very little about P so set about educating ourselves by talking to a drug counsellor with the Salvation Army in Dunedin, visiting our local doctor, and also contacting the local AA group. When Jacob rang us we were well prepared.

He spoke softly, as though he was afraid to do so. He was obviously ashamed of his situation and reluctant to open up.

'Jacob, if you want to come and live with us, we need to discuss some rules. Are you up for that?' I asked, tackling the situation head on.

'Yes,' he said quietly.

'Firstly, tell me why you want to come down and live here with us.'

'I need to get out of home and out of Wellington. It is too easy to get drugs here.'

Lance was listening in, as we knew this had to be a family decision. We would all have to share the weight of Jacob's journey to recovery.

'Listen, Jacob, when it comes to smoking, I am an addict,' Lance said. 'I have tried more times than I can count to stop, but I still smoke. Breaking an addiction is hard — this is going to be a tough time. Are you ready for that?'

Lance was right — he had tried many times to quit smoking, sometimes stopping for months, but to me it seemed like he was always waiting for an excuse to start again. I desperately wanted him to stop, even threatening to leave him if he didn't. At one point I wrote him this letter:

> *Like a lover you caress her in your hand many times a day, her taste lingers on your lips, your tongue, and on your breath. She walks with you everywhere.*
>
> *She has totally possessed you, never leaving your side, controlling your mind, your moods and your entire day. You willingly give her your money, bend to her every need, and fret when you think you have lost her for just a few minutes. Even with your complete dedication, she does not love you. She has convinced you that you need her to exist.*
>
> *I have been there, beside you, watching every manipulative move, trying to live with you . . . and her. I smell her on you every minute I am with you, always aware of her presence. I witness her demands and your blind loving response. Even when you speak to me, she is there, sometimes as blatant as the fine sliver of paper stuck to your lower lip, or a grey mist creeping from your mouth.*
>
> *I sit alone while you walk with her, hungrily kiss her, soak in her very essence. I wait, anger welling up in me until I want to scream. I make excuses for you*

— hurting when friends tell me the obvious. Your life is being sucked out of you as her fingers of death creep into every cell of your body, yet you cling to her as though your life depends on her. An honest man turned into a man who schemes, is dishonest and deceitful, just to be with her. You have told me 'to get a life' when I have dared to mention her, even when realising that she has taken so much from us and is taking your life away.

There is no laughter left in me as I witness this affair. No longer do I want to make love to you, as she seeps into me, your silent partner, her poison making me choke. My back is turned towards you as we lie in bed, yet I yearn for your touch, your tenderness, and your love. My dreams are of your death . . . even then she is at your bedside holding your hand.

I have written what I cannot say for fear of reproach, the flash of anger and raised voice. She is never to be criticised, or discussed? Her continual presence must never be acknowledged. I have written this to try and get my life back with you, without her. Inside I am weeping as I realise I can no longer live this way. She has finally won, I am no longer competition.

The decision was yours, now it is mine.

In the end I stayed. If I wanted a life with Lance, I had to accept his addiction.

'Jacob, are you up for this?' Lance asked again.

'Yes I am.' He sounded firmer this time.

'Great, then we'll give it a go, but here are the rules. No drugs or alcohol. You have to attend an AA meeting every week. You will do work around our property to pay your way until you are fit enough to find a job.'

We were also keen that Jacob's mother attend AA or NA (Narcotics Anonymous) because she was a heavy dope smoker and we were convinced that was part of Jacob's problem. We spoke to Andrew about that, and also Jacob's mother, but ultimately we couldn't force her to do anything she didn't want to do.

'I definitely want to come down if you will have me,' Jacob said.

'Great, then get yourself down here,' I said. 'We love you no matter what. This is going to be hard for all of us but we can do it, and so can you.'

—

A COUPLE OF WEEKS later Jacob flew into Invercargill, looking pale, tired and scared. As I hugged him I felt him go stiff and pull away. 'You'll have to get used to hugging,' I told him. 'It's what we do.'

He nodded.

The drive from Invercargill to Manapōuri is just under two hours and Jacob slept most of the way. Even in his sleep his face looked strained.

He moved into our small self-contained flat next door. We left him to unpack and settle in, telling him to come over for dinner around six.

There was a quiet knock on the door. 'Come in, Jacob. No need to knock. You're part of the family.'

'I didn't want to be rude,' he replied in a quiet voice.

After dinner we went through the rules again and laid out clearly what we expected of him. The local doctor had told us that initially Jacob wouldn't be able to do much physical work, and that he would want to sleep a lot. We explained that we had just had two large pine trees felled in our forest and Lance had cut the trunks into rings. Jacob's job was to cut them up into firewood. We didn't mind how long it took, so long as he did a little each day.

A couple of days later we heard wood being chopped. There was our grandson swinging an axe. It looked like very hard work as he had yet to gain the skills he needed. Lance stepped alongside him and talked about wood grain, how to swing an axe correctly, how to stand, and how to roll and lift the rings. This was the first bonding opportunity for the two of them.

Early on, we took Jacob to the doctor for a checkup. As far as he could tell, Jacob showed no lasting effects from his P use, but the doctor suggested a trip to the dentist.

On the first Tuesday night I drove Jacob to his first AA meeting, as there was no Narcotics Anonymous meeting in Te Anau at the time. I had checked this out with them beforehand. We were made very welcome, and although Jacob spent the entire meeting looking down at his feet, he was taking it all in. Meeting participants were supportive and over the next few weeks he was encouraged to join in. It took time, but progress was being made.

By the end of the first month Jacob was out chopping and splitting wood all day, stopping only for lunch or a drink, or to feed the chickens. He finished each day exhausted, but had grown to really enjoy the challenge. We were now hugging frequently, and speaking openly. It was a joy to see him laughing.

It was time to give him another challenge.

'How about I teach you to shoot rabbits?' Lance asked.

'Really? That would be great.'

'Come on, then. We'll go down and sight the rifle, make sure it's shooting straight.'

Jacob was excited as they drove down to the rifle range. This was completely outside his experience.

From then on they went rabbit shooting nearly every evening, always coming home full of stories and proudly bringing back the carcasses for the hawks that come and feed in our back yard.

It was time for another life lesson.

'What we shoot, we should use, Jacob,' Lance told him.

'We don't kill for the fun of it. Ruth is going to roast a rabbit for dinner tonight.'

Jacob looked at me in disbelief. 'I'm not going to eat rabbit!'

'Why not?'

'I don't know — it might make us sick.'

'We can safely eat almost anything we kill — rabbits, deer, fish, wild pigs.'

Next, Lance taught him to skin a rabbit. 'You kill it, you skin it,' he said. Jacob was apprehensive, but with guidance he slowly learnt the skill.

—

WE DROVE TO Invercargill to see a dentist, and we had also made an appointment with a drug counsellor at the hospital. There was some work needed on his teeth but not as much as Jacob — and we — had feared.

'I thought I might teach you how to fish for trout,' Lance said to Jacob one day.

'Sounds great. When?'

Lance set up a fishing line and away they went in our dinghy down the Waiau River. After their first catch Lance showed him how to take the hook out of the fish's mouth, how to kill it quickly and humanely, and how to gut it.

Jacob then hooked a trout. 'Your fish — you have to kill it,' said Lance.

'*No!* I can't!'

'Then you shouldn't be fishing. Treat the fish with respect and do it quickly.'

Lance stood back as Jacob killed the fish. When they arrived home he proudly showed me his beautiful trout, which was gutted and ready to cook. As we ate it, I asked, 'How does it feel to be bringing food home for the table?' He smiled, but wouldn't go as far as saying he liked the idea.

JACOB HAD BEEN with us for nearly two months without touching drugs or alcohol and we thought he was well enough to look for paid work. We suggested he look for something local so he could walk to work.

A lot of the work down our way is in the tourism industry, so we gave him some advice. 'Before we can recommend you to an employer we need you to commit to working the full tourist season. It's a big ask, but a lot of doors in the industry will close to you permanently if you leave part-way through the season. It will also make local employers less likely to accept recommendations from us in future.' We believed he was up to it.

Jacob wasn't as confident as we were. 'I don't know if I can work a full week. What if I let you down?'

I gave him a hug. 'We believe you can do it, love. Trust yourself.'

We encouraged him to line up an interview, give it his best shot, and take it from there. 'You have the skills; so go for it.'

His hair was tidy, his skin had cleared, and he was wearing his good clothes. He looked great as he set off. We waited for him to come home.

'I start next week in the office!' He was so happy.

A day or two later he went grocery shopping with Lance in Te Anau, and on the way home they came across a road-kill deer. Lance was excited at the chance to teach Jacob how to skin a deer and cut off the back steaks. After dropping off the groceries they headed back to the deer, taking plastic bags and a large sharp knife.

Lance knew from looking at the deer that it had been dead for a while, and we likely wouldn't be able to eat the meat, but it was a great opportunity to pass on more country skills to Jacob, who was no longer such a city boy.

They dragged the carcass off to the side of the road and Lance set to work. He sliced the belly skin in order to gut the animal, carefully avoiding rupturing the stomach. This is not normally a smelly job but, in this case, the whole stomach area had been mangled by the impact of the car. The smell was so overwhelming that Jacob started to retch, and Lance admitted later that he was also on the verge of vomiting, but he kept going, eager for the lesson not to be wasted.

The meat was badly bruised and too far gone to bring

home so in the end he only removed the back steaks. By now Jacob was standing about 3 metres away, looking ashen. 'Are we really going to eat that?' he asked.

'We'll give it a go and see what it's like.'

Although the meat was well past being edible, it was an experience that Jacob would never forget, and a memory we often recall and laugh about.

—

HE DID EXCEPTIONALLY well at work, and within a few weeks was given more responsibility, including opening up in the morning. The women in the office really liked him. What was not to like? He was good-looking, gentle, hardworking and considerate.

We started to call him Magnet Man, since his workmates kept bringing him lunch, inviting him out and quite often turning up on his doorstep to visit.

Some months later I was moving our car out onto the road when I saw an attractive young woman come out of Jacob's flat. She had beautiful long hair and a friendly face, and was confident when she spoke.

'Hi, so you are Jacob's girlfriend?' I smiled at her.

She smiled back and introduced herself as Rebecca. Over the following weeks we got to know her quite well. She knew Jacob's history and was understanding and supportive. At the end of the tourist season they holidayed together around New Zealand before they both travelled to her homeland in Europe.

—

FIVE YEARS LATER Jacob is in his last year of a building apprenticeship. Yes, he has had the odd brief relapse, but we could not be prouder of our grandson. We know that the hook of addiction will always be with him, just as it is with Lance, and thousands of others.

TALES FROM THE BOOKSHOPS: ONE HAND CLAPPING

TWO WOMEN CAME into the shop and we started chatting. Jacqui was from Tauranga, down visiting her lifelong friend Trish, who had recently moved with her husband to Te Anau.

Jacqui was a big reader and was looking for a book for herself. 'I read in your book that you have the knack of choosing the right book for anyone who comes in!' she said.

I asked what sorts of books she liked.

'Historical fiction,' she replied.

A copy of the wonderful book *The Sound of One Hand Clapping* by Richard Flanagan (1997) had come in only a couple of days before. The title is an adaptation of a statement made by the great Japanese Zen master Hakuin Ekaku (1685–1768) to challenge and provoke his students. He said: 'Two hands clap and there is a sound, what is the sound of one hand?'

I don't know why I lifted this book off the shelf, as it is not historical fiction, but I handed it to Jacqui, saying, 'I think you'll really like this book.'

She read the title and, with a look of surprise, handed it to her friend. They both gasped.

'What's wrong?' I asked.

Jacqui looked at me. 'My husband has only one arm and he tells me he can do everything but clap.'

I couldn't believe it. Out of all the books I could have chosen, this was the one that had stood out.

I had to know the backstory of Greig, her husband. (And yes, Greig is the correct spelling — it was his Scottish mother's maiden name.)

At the age of 12, Greig bought his first motorbike for £2. He spent another £9 to get it up and running, and sold it for £6. Not the greatest of business ventures! Over the next few years he owned 29 different bikes, mainly English models, then in 1969 he bought his first Honda. He quickly progressed to a Honda 750 cc, one of the first of 30 that were imported into Auckland.

Up until the age of 20, Greig had never had an accident, but in 1971 he collided with another bike. He smashed one arm and one leg, and broke several teeth. As well, the nerves running from the spine to his right arm were ripped out.

The result was 56 stitches in his face, several days in a coma, and 13 weeks in hospital. Greig carried his arm in a sling for about two years before it had to be amputated.

He suffered severe phantom pain after this surgery, and was living on painkillers.

Eight years after the amputation he met a surgeon who thought he might be able to reduce the amount of pain Greig was experiencing.

Greig watched on an X-ray screen as dye was injected into

his spine to identify the nerve damage. When it reached the top of his neck they sat him up, explaining that it would be dangerous if it reached his brain. He had to remain vertical for the next 24 hours. Two days later they operated, opening up two vertebrae, sealing nerve endings and then wiring everything back together.

The outcome was that the level of Greig's phantom pain was reduced. Although it is still constant, it is at a level he can handle.

The transition to being left-handed was challenging and far-reaching. Greig had completed his plumber's trade certificate before the accident, receiving his pass while still in hospital, but had only completed 9500 hours of his 10,000-hour apprenticeship. After a long battle with the apprenticeship board, the remaining 500 hours were credited.

Even though he could no longer perform the physical work of plumbing, Greig became the office manager for a plumbing firm. Nothing stood in his way as he went to Australia with some mates to work in the mines, returned home and started work with a building company where he stayed for 35 years.

So if anyone will understand the title of the book *The Sound of One Hand Clapping*, it is Greig. It is about facing challenges, approaching problems from a different perspective, and being able to adapt. That is exactly what Greig's story is all about.

CHAPTER
23

COVE'S LAST CHAPTER

My office is full of books, boxes, files and knick-knacks. A pile of hats sits comfortably on top of one of the bookshelves, and rolls of Raeco for covering the dust jackets of the more expensive books, together with piles of recycled paper bags, top even more bookshelves. Floor space is limited but there is always room for Cove, our part-time dog, who is my writing buddy.

From the time I started to write *The Bookseller at the End of the World*, Cove decided he would lie down beside my chair, just to be with me. Even at five in the morning, when Lance would get up with me to light the fire and make me a cup of coffee before I started writing, Cove would follow me into my office. With a sigh he would drop his beautiful head on my lap so I could rub his velvety black ears, then lie down and fall asleep. He was ready for a few hours of writing.

Many readers will know about Cove from my two previous books. He was on the cover of *Bookshop Dogs* — the black and white dog with the stunned look on his face, his ears sticking out like two bird wings.

Cove came into our lives in 2015, a quiet, well-behaved eight-year-old dog whose owner, Regan, goes to sea for up to 10 days at a time, so we are Cove's minders in his absence.

Now at the ripe old age of 17, Cove has dementia, is totally deaf, and has arthritis in his back legs and lower spine. His beautiful white paws are splayed. He can no longer bark, he has cataracts, and he only wags his tail at mealtimes, or when someone gives him a cuddle. Increasingly, he is having difficulty standing up. Regan often carries him to and from his car into our home, or from his mat to the grass for a pee.

TODAY IS A DAY I will always remember. This morning Regan, Lance and I decided it was time to farewell our incredible Cove. As I type the final episode in his story he is lying asleep beside my chair, in one of his happy places. The only sounds I can hear are the tapping of the computer keys and the occasional soft snore from the floor.

The discussion this morning was difficult. We were all crying as we acknowledged that Cove's quality of life had deteriorated so much that we could no longer put off the tough decision. The vet is to arrive at 4 p.m.

We are each getting through his final hours in our own way. Regan bought Cove a whole roast chicken, and we have been giving him yummy treats most of the day. His coat is black and shiny as Regan gave him a bath. With all this fuss, I wonder if he knows something important is going to happen today.

Over the last 10 years we have been looking after Cove he has given us so much. His younger days were spent digging up buried bones, greeting customers at the bookshops, or just dog-napping in the sunshine with an eye half open to everything going on around him. We nicknamed him the million-dollar dog for the amount Regan shelled out to the vet — one operation cost around $10,000!

He went through a stage of being constantly constipated, then he developed paraphimosis — an inability to completely retract the penis. To help him I had to slip on a pair of rubber gloves, smooth a cream over his penis and gently push it back into place. I became an expert at this over the months he had this condition.

The dementia, which is not uncommon in old dogs, has made him insecure, especially if he can't see us. It means he wants to be with us all the time. Even when I'm doing my exercises in the morning he will lie down beside me, often with his head near my chest so he can look directly at my eyes. When I finish my floor exercises and stand up to do more, Cove also stands, and pads over to his bed to watch me from there.

—

REGAN'S PARTNER EMMA is driving from Frankton, near Queenstown, to be here by four o'clock. She also wants to say goodbye to Cove. Meanwhile, I write.

Cove now has his head resting on my lap, after pushing his nose up under my arm for attention and a rub on the head. He looks me straight in the eye. I stop writing and talk to him. He listens. I am sure he understands so I am careful with my words.

'You are such a brilliant dog, Cove. You have been with me while I have written nearly three books. You have snuggled up to me when I have cried, letting me know you are there for me. I will be finishing this book without you by my side, but I will never forget you.' He blinks and slowly lies back down, slipping into the calmness of sleep. I cannot imagine him not being here, always by my side, always in my way.

Jill, the vet, arrives with a nurse. Both have known Cove for many years. He is on his bed, polishing off the last of his roast chicken, as Jill tries to find a vein to inject the sedative. His veins have collapsed but Jill is experienced, and within a short time Cove is snoring. He feels nothing as the euthanasia medication is administered, slipping gently from sleep into nothingness.

Jill and the nurse leave us alone to say our final goodbyes. Regan, Emma and I are crying. Lance holds me; his tears will come later.

—

DAYS LATER, REGAN arrives with a small cardboard box carrying Cove's ashes. They will sit in my office so I can see them as I write. We receive a beautiful card from the vet clinic with a copy of Cove's pawprint attached. There are more tears as memories flood back.

Just over a week later I am speaking at the Invercargill Library. I have to talk about *Bookshop Dogs* but I know I can't mention Cove's name, or I'll lose it. So I read a chapter about Hunza, our small German shepherd, who died nearly 30 years ago.

In closing, I read about a wee dog that visits me occasionally. I don't know anything about her, except that she randomly turns up, accepts a small treat and then trots off, head held high. I start to cry as I read and I can't stop; the pain is still too raw. I know everyone will understand, and I see some of the audience are also crying.

Almost everyone present will have lost their best friend, the companion who accepted them no matter what, or maybe accompanied them to work every morning to help share the load. One woman tells me she had to put her dog down only a week before, and as I sit to sign copies of *Bookshop Dogs*, I listen to the stories of other precious, well-loved dogs that will never be forgotten.

It is never really goodbye. As I write, I miss Cove lying beside me. I miss the comfort of his soft, slow snore and the rhythm of his breathing. I have no one to read to when I finish a chapter; my words now fall into an empty space.

Tears slip silently down my cheeks. There is nothing more to say.

TALES FROM THE BOOKSHOPS: LIFE LESSONS FOR LEX

—

YOU MAY HAVE read about Lex in my first book. He was only six years old then and desperately wanted to be my 'assistant'. This arrangement lasted for about two weeks.

'Hi, Ruth. I'm going fishing with Dad so I can't work.'

'Okay. When will you be back?'

'Don't know.' Off he went on his bike with a big smile.

When I reopened the following season he came to see me.

'I can help you,' he announced.

'I have another assistant; in fact he is my apprentice,' I informed him.

'What's that?'

I explained what an apprentice was and told him Dylan would be working a day a week.

'What about me?'

'You stopped turning up for work so I assumed you had left. Lucky I didn't buy you a computer or set you up with a desk!'

'I didn't leave. I had to work with Dad, opening and closing the farm gates. And we went fishing — and duck shooting.'

'You have been busy, but sorry, Dylan has your job now.'

With a shrug of his shoulders he raced off on his bike.

Two days later Lex came running down our path, one side of his head covered in blood.

'*Lex!* What happened?'

'Got attacked by a pig!' he exclaimed.

'Don't tell lies, Lex. Come and show me your head.' He approached and proudly displayed his injury. It wasn't pretty. 'You'd better go home and show your mother,' I said. 'It needs to be cleaned up and possibly stitched.'

About half an hour later Lex was back, with his mother in tow. He ran over to show me his head. The wound was now clean and his hair was no longer stuck to his head with blood.

'It looks great, Lex. Much better. What happened, Sarah?' I turned to his mum.

'A pig attacked him.'

'Told you! Told you!' yelled Lex.

CHAPTER
24

IT'S NOT EASY BEING GREEN

I was invited to speak at a New Zealand Tourism event in 1999. At the time, eco-tourism was seen as a new and exciting way to protect the environment, and Fiordland Ecology Holidays had just won the national eco-tourism award for a second time.

The 100% *Pure New Zealand* marketing campaign had been launched that year, and many (including us) disputed the claim. We believed the New Zealand environment, its lakes and rivers and oceans, were well short of 100 per cent pure, and much more needed to be done. Going against the hype, we spoke out about the importance of protecting the environment, and said we would not be adopting the slogan *100% Pure* in any of our advertising.

We were dismissed as 'greenies' — sandal-wearing, long-haired dope smokers. Tree huggers.

I opened my speech with the following:

'Joe Raposo wrote the famous song "It's Not Easy Being Green", which was sung by Jim Henderson as Kermit the Frog in *Sesame Street* and *The Muppets*. It quickly became Kermit's signature song.' I quoted them (but didn't sing!) a couple of verses.

I told the awards event attendees that New Zealand tourism operators needed to establish strong, bold guidelines that showed we were serious about the environment. This meant a complete turnaround in how operators structured their businesses, and for many years we had all placed this in the too-hard basket. But our bank was Mother Nature, not the Bank of New Zealand or the ANZ, as without caring for her, we would go bankrupt.

Standing up for the environment was not — and still isn't — easy. For charter vessel operators throughout New Zealand, fishing is their main drawcard, and around the country — and the world — fish stocks have collapsed due to overfishing.

This is why Fiordland Ecology Holidays adopted a 'no fishing' policy for our charters. Our accountant and lawyer thought we were doomed to fail but still supported us.

We proved them wrong. We remained profitable, we were now winning eco-tourism awards, and *Breaksea Girl* was always fully booked months in advance.

Our focus was environmental education, and that meant telling the hard facts — that our country was not 100 per cent pure. Native forests in Fiordland were not 'untouched' — they were being decimated by introduced predators. Fish stocks were depleted to the extent that recreational fishing inside the fiords was now unsustainable, and some of our lakes and rivers were slippery with the invasive algae didymo, for which there was no known cure. Nature was hanging on by a thread.

—

FOR THOSE OF US who were born just after the war, the words conservation and environment were hardly ever mentioned when we were growing up. We swam in streams and rivers with crystal-clear water; we'd never heard of sunblock; there was always enough fish to catch for a meal; the sandy beaches were full of pipi and cockles.

We survived without plastic bags, which didn't appear until the 1960s. We knew nothing of the havoc being caused in the bush and forests by rats, mice, stoats, deer, rabbits and possums. There always seemed to be enough of everything. Our generation was lucky.

I read *Silent Spring* by Rachel Carson, published in

1962, and it opened my eyes. I joined the Save the Whales campaign and found myself marching in the streets with hundreds of other concerned people. I felt passionate, but also saddened as I started to research what was really happening all around the world. Our natural world was under serious threat.

I wrote letters to governments all over the world pleading for the protection of animals, birds and old-growth forests, and begging them to protect native tribes being driven from their ancestral lands. It was never-ending. Forty years ago I wrote to the government of Malta pleading with them to stop the slaughter of migrating birds. Nothing has changed — the Maltese government still uses a loophole in the European Union's Birds Directive to allow the practice of hunting migratory birds that touch down in Malta en route from Africa to Europe. The environmental organisation BirdLife Malta believes that over 7000 birds per square kilometre are killed in Malta every year.

Being an environmentalist means you sometimes have to accept you are fighting a losing battle, which is exhausting, infuriating and often expensive. No matter what your cause, you have to do your homework; your facts have to be 100 per cent correct, because you will be challenged every step of the way. The occasional win keeps you going, but then there can be a change of government and the gains you have made are overthrown.

The small shed in our back yard is full of records of

various environmental battles I've been involved in over the years, in New Zealand and Australia. We lost a lot of them, but we did win some:

- We stopped a dam being built on the Franklin River in Tasmania.
- We stopped raw sewage being pumped into the sea near Bondi Beach, Sydney.
- Together with Earthtrust and Greenpeace, we had drift-netting banned in southern oceans.
- We stopped large tankers coming into Doubtful Sound to extract fresh water from the tailrace — and we did it twice, as after the first application was turned down the company went bankrupt, only to reapply under another name.
- We gained protection for red coral (along with black coral) in Fiordland.
- A group of energetic women named the Bee Gees (yes, we did get their permission to use their name!) cleared stoat and rat traps on a section of the Kepler Track for many years.
- We stopped cruise ships coming into the head of Doubtful Sound.
- We helped stop commercial extraction of sea cucumbers from Fiordland.
- A group of concerned tourism operators worked together with DOC to establish strict guidelines to

protect the resident pod of bottle-nosed dolphins in Doubtful Sound.

- Several groups, including Save Fiordland (Te Anau) and Stop the Tunnel Group (Glenorchy), managed to defeat a plan to build a $240 million monorail through Fiordland National Park.
- Floating hotels were banned inside the fiords.
- Jet-skis were banned inside the fiords.
- The number of surface-water consents in Fiordland was restricted, reducing the number of charter vessels permitted to operate.
- In 2000 Lance and I established the Breaksea Conservation Fund to finance environmental projects. A percentage of our company profits went into the fund and many of our clients made donations after learning about our work. In 2005 one of the projects we initiated was to clear Pomona Island and Rona Island (in Lake Manapōuri) of predators. Once this was achieved, Haast tokoeka kiwi were introduced.

The real biggie for me was when concerned residents from Manapōuri formed Fiordland Sewage Options to oppose the Southland District Council's plan to discharge semi-treated sewage via rotary irrigators onto land beside the Te Anau–Manapōuri Airport.

I was their spokesperson and joint chair, together with

Alistair Paton-McDonald, known to all as Furrie. Our concerns were many: the obvious health and safety issues associated with sewage; the potential degradation of water quality in both the Waiau River and Lake Manapōuri; groundwater contamination; tourist perceptions of the idea of semi-treated human wastewater being sprayed at the gateway to a World Heritage park; the risk of bird strike at the nearby airport — to name but a few.

It started when, in January 2015, after two years of opposition, a 25-year consent was granted to the Southland District Council permitting partially treated effluent from Te Anau to be piped 20 km to a site close to the township of Manapōuri and bordering the airport. It would then be sprayed onto the land through aerial irrigators, bringing further concerns of odour and spray drift.

We appealed the decision, taking it to the Environment Court and raising over $100,000 to do so. Our consultant presented four fully costed alternatives, all of which we believed had better cultural, environmental, financial and social outcomes as they incorporated the latest technologies.

Subsurface irrigation was the obvious option. We would still have the pipeline, but the effluent would be treated to a far higher standard and discharged through a series of buried perforated polyethylene driplines. The roots of planted crops would take up the moisture, and when harvested result in an income for the council.

But the commissioner declined to rule one way or the other, telling us to sort it with the council.

When I had been involved in the fight to stop raw sewage being pumped into the ocean near Bondi Beach, we raised our profile enormously when our theme song hit the streets, and this is what I sang to the SDC when I told them this was not my first poo fight:

Oh I do like to be beside the seaside,
I do like to be beside the sea.
I do like to walk upon hypodermic needles
Picking up a nasty dose of hepatitis B.
Oh! I do like to walk among the condoms,
The bacteria and poo,
But walking naked in the sun
With melanomas on my bum
Is what I really like to do!

I was ready for a long, hard fight. *We* were ready for the fight. I collected sewage samples from the treatment ponds in Te Anau. The public had been assured that the discharge from the aerial irrigators was 'nearly as good as drinking water', so let them prove it.

I carefully poured the yellow-green fluid into small bio-hazard containers, sealed the tops and handed them out to councillors at the next meeting. 'This is what you are going to spray on the people of Manapōuri,' I told them.

When one councillor refused to accept his container, saying he had children at home, I looked at him and said, 'I rest my case!'

Finally, after seven years, the council agreed to subsurface irrigation. The small group of us who made up Fiordland Sewage Options could not believe it was over. We had achieved so much. I even got to cut the ribbon to officially open the new subsoil irrigation plant. On 7 October 2022 the *Southland Times* reported:

> *Ruth Shaw was not taking Te Anau's crap, and she eventually got her way.*
>
> *The Manapouri resident fought the Southland District Council for years over its proposal to spray Te Anau's treated sewage onto land beside the Te Anau–Manapouri Airport, just 4km from her hometown . . .*
>
> *The official opening [of the new subsoil irrigation plant], which Southland district councillors attended together with a large crowd of invited residents, was carried out by Ruth Shaw and Alistair Paton-McDonald, who jointly chair Fiordland Sewage Options, as well as Mayor Gary Tong and deputy mayor Ebel Kremer who stated: 'It's certainly the way forward for wastewater plants for the future. The*

> *days of just pumping wastewater into our waterways [are] pretty well over.'*

The Te Anau–Manapōuri wastewater scheme is now recognised by other councils as the way forward for treating and discharging wastewater.

But that's not the end of the story, alas. Our small township of Manapōuri is now faced with having to upgrade its own sewage treatment plant. At least now subsurface irrigation is an industry standard, but as a conservationist you never take anything for granted.

TALES FROM THE BOOKSHOPS: MONET'S GARDEN

LINNEA IN MONET'S GARDEN, a small, beautiful children's book written by Christina Björk and illustrated by Lena Anderson, was published in Sweden in 1985 and translated into English soon after. A copy arrived on my desk together with a pile of other children's books. I cleaned it, checked it for damage and then read it, finding it suitable for young readers over seven years of age.

It was different from any other children's book I had in stock. As I placed it on the shelf, I wondered who would buy it . . . someone interested in art, maybe?

It is a story about a young girl named Linnea, who, together with her Uncle Blomkvist, goes on an adventure to Giverny in Paris, where they visit the garden of painter Claude Monet. The cover drawing shows Linnea standing on the little Japanese bridge that Monet painted so often in his work.

During their visit Linnea sees many of Monet's paintings, which are themselves beautifully illustrated throughout the book. By the end of the story she understands what it means to be called an Impressionist, and she has learnt about Monet's life in the pink house where he lived with two of his own children and the six offspring of his second wife.

Within a week a young woman was standing at my desk clutching *Linnea in Monet's Garden*. She had a huge smile — it was as though she had found something precious that had been lost for a long time.

'So, you've found the book on Monet's paintings. Isn't it exquisite?'

'It is incredible that this book is here,' she replied. 'I have stood on that bridge.' She pointed to the cover picture. 'I have walked up that pathway and visited Monet's home — this is amazing!'

She pulled her phone out of her pocket and showed me the photos. 'And look, here is the garden, the waterlily pond, the pathway, and his home. I have been there! This book was meant for me.'

Her name was Chloe, and, like Linnea, she loved Monet's paintings — his obvious love of nature and his use of soft, warm colours.

Under the Nazi regime, Jewish art collectors in German-occupied countries were systematically looted by the Nazis and their agents. Thousands of artworks valued at many millions of euros were plundered, and many have never been recovered.

As recently as 2023 a Monet pastel drawing, *Bord de Mer*, which had belonged to Austrian couple Adalbert and Hilda Parlagi in the 1930s, was found by the FBI in private hands. The Parlagis had stored the work with the rest of their belongings when they fled Vienna to escape the Nazis, but German authorities had helped themselves and the artwork made its way to an auction house owned by Nazi art 'looter' Adolf Weinmüller. It has since been returned to the owners' descendants.

Chloe and I talked about her visit to Monet's garden. She was clearly the perfect person to own this book. Like Monet's *Bord de Mer*, the small book had found a safe home.

CHAPTER
25

THE OLD WOMAN AT THE END OF THE WORLD

By the time this book is published I will be 79.

Our South African friend Michael, who is a clinical psychologist, once told me about the 'half-dead parties' he and his friends held when they turned 35. The idea stemmed from the biblical idea of a full life being 'three score years and ten', after which 'we fly away'.

Well, Lance has already reached *four* score years (plus one), and I am well over the biblical lifespan, so we will soon be flying away. I hope it's not too soon, as I still have so much more to squeeze in . . .

My brain has slowed down considerably. Where once I could read a document and remember most of it, now I have to read it three or four times. My body is slowly shrinking — I am a bag of wrinkles and I appear to have too much skin; age spots keep appearing; my fingers are lumpy with arthritis; and it costs a fortune to keep my teeth looking presentable. So yes, I am now an old woman. I can no longer consider myself middle-aged-creeping-towards-old-age. I am already there.

Jack, aged nine, has been coming into the Children's Bookshop since he was five. During the last Christmas holidays he turned up with his cousin of a similar age, but as I was busy in the main shop I didn't have a chance to say hello. It didn't matter. He glanced inside and I heard him tell his friend, 'It's all right, we can go into our bookshop. The old lady is busy but she won't mind.'

He usually calls me Ruth so I had to smile when I heard this. When my other customers had left, carrying a bag of books, I went over to the Children's Bookshop to see Jack and his cousin.

'Hi, Ruth, this is Henry,' Jack said as he looked up.

Cutting straight to the point, I asked, 'How old do you think I am, Jack?'

His face was serious while he studied me. 'Older than my mum, but not as old as my grandmother, who is really, *really* old. So just old.'

Confirmation received!

Maybe it is time for Lance and me to hold a 'very nearly dead' party.

—

MY LIFE HAS changed considerably since my first book was published in 2022. I am overwhelmed, grateful and incredibly humbled by the attention my books have brought me. I never expected this to happen, as most of my life I have found myself standing alone, fighting for my corner. Thankfully I have had the resilience and determination to stand by my beliefs, and now I also have Lance as my wingman, supporting me, as he promised when we got married.

Over a hundred years ago a French philosopher, writer and political activist named Simone Weil published an essay called 'The Power of Words', written when she was just 25. She firmly believed that words could have strength, but could also be rendered hollow, particularly by politicians. She was right. Sadly, she died very young, at the age of 34.

I have always been aware of the power of words. I excelled in English, but failed maths and history. I learnt at an early age that I could swing a decision or influence a debate through the strength of my words.

The Bookseller at the End of the World touched readers in many different ways. It empowered abused women and men to find a voice; it helped readers find courage and realise they could survive trauma.

I never expected my second book, *Bookshop Dogs*, to have any such impact — it was basically a series of stories about dogs and their owners, and about our wonderful Hunza.

I was wrong.

Alice Harris, a teacher at Hauroko Valley Primary School in rural Southland, emailed to thank me for writing *Bookshop Dogs*, which she was reading to her pupils. She asked if it might be possible for them to come and meet me.

After numerous emails it was organised. The children were apparently loving the dog stories so I arranged for a number of the dogs mentioned in the book to come and join in the fun.

On the day, 42 school children, along with sundry parents, turned up in a long chain of cars. Alice was exactly how I had imagined her — energetic, well organised, gentle but firm: exactly the type of teacher I wished I had had when I was at school. We all squeezed into the Manapōuri Boating Club Hall, many of the children sitting on floor mats, the adults on chairs. *Dog Day* had arrived!

Graham Dainty, who took the photographs for the book, introduced his dog Shady Lady, along with Hank, Sam, Ellie, Cane, Pippa, Gypsy, Berri and Bill — and their owners. (Stella couldn't come as she had toothache and had to go to the vet.)

The children had brought fantastic drawings of nearly all the dogs in the book. As each owner finished speaking to the assembled group, they were given a drawing of their dog, presented by the young artist.

I'll never forget *Dog Day*. My words had not only been read, but had touched the lives of these children. I wanted to cry as I watched them with the dogs — the excitement, their concern, love and gentleness. I managed to hold back my tears until Lance and I finally waved goodbye to the parade of cars filled with excited 'readers' dressed in school uniform.

—

'DID YOU HAVE a lovely day today?' I ask Lance.

He smiles and answers with his own question. 'Are you happy with your life?' (He's fond of the saying 'happy wife, happy life'.)

We ask each other this question often, and most of the time the answer is yes. How wonderful is that?

If you have read my first book you will know that the roadmap of my life has not been an open highway. More like a series of rutted dirt tracks, often with locked gates along the way. On these tracks I survived the harshness of life and the darkest of nights. Yes, I have survived. I found courage and unconditional love.

This story is finished. I go to my library, select a book, settle into my favourite seat and open the first chapter …

I am in my happy place.

ACKNOWLEDGEMENTS

WHAT GOES ON behind every book before it reaches the shelves of bookshops? You will possibly know the author; you may take notice of the artwork on the cover, but what about the artist and the designer? Who has carefully edited and proofread the book? Who has worked hard to get it in the hands of readers? You might glance at who the publishers are, not realising that there is a bevy of incredible people beavering away behind the scenes to ensure the book is successful.

The team at Allen & Unwin have my back: they care for me and Lance, support us, and ensure we are part of their 'family'. I wonder how many writers have received a food parcel from their publishers after falling sick? Special thanks to Abba from publicity and marketing, who is always there for me, together with Jenny, my publisher. Thanks also to my editor, Rachel Scott, for her care and attention. My books would not be as successful as they are without the whole team, and saying 'thank you' does not even come close to capturing how I feel about you all.

When Jeongeun Shin from South Korea emailed me and said she was going to establish a publishing company so she could translate and publish my first book, I was overwhelmed. What courage! Thank you sincerely, Jeongeun.

There are many others to thank: my long-suffering friends and family, my bookshop helpers who are a joy to work with, and of course my wingman: my amazing husband, Lance. He is always beside me, bringing me back onto a safe course when I start to doubt myself and my writing.

And then there is you, my reader. Thank you for your incredible support; your love, hugs and understanding. I write with you all sitting beside me, aware that the power of words cannot be taken lightly.

A virtual hug to you all.

Ruth